The Standard

Christian Epidemic

The Standard Christian Epidemic

By David Vilkhovoy

WESTBOW
PRESS
A DIVISION OF THOMAS NELSON

WestBow Press books may be ordered through booksellers or by contacting:

WestBow Press
A Division of Thomas Nelson
1663 Liberty Drive
Bloomington, IN 47403
www.westbowpress.com
1-(866) 928-1240

Because of the dynamic nature of the Internet, any web addresses or links contained in this book may have changed since publication and may no longer be valid. The views expressed in this work are solely those of the author and do not necessarily reflect the views of the publisher, and the publisher hereby disclaims any responsibility for them.

Any people depicted in stock imagery provided by Thinkstock are models, and such images are being used for illustrative purposes only.

Certain stock imagery © Thinkstock.

ISBN: 978-1-4497-8178-1 (sc)
ISBN: 978-1-4497-8179-8 (e)

Library of Congress Control Number: 2013900384

Printed in the United States of America

WestBow Press rev. date: 2/8/2013

Dedication

I dedicate this book to Christians everywhere, that they would represent Jesus Christ as the author and finisher of their faith, not allowing any man to tempt them with religion.

Acknowledgements

Mom— Thank you for loving me unconditionally and always stirring the fire of God within me.

Dad—Thank you for believing in me and always being patient with me. You shaped me into the man I am today.

Grandma Nina—You raised me since I was a child in the ways of God. I am forever grateful to your love and discipline.

Alex—As your younger brother, I have matured and grown by your example throughout the years. You've always been the role model I needed in my life.

Tatyana— Although you have gone home, your life lives on through me. Thank you for setting the first example of a Christ-like attitude in our home. I am forever changed by you.

Vika—To whom do I owe as much love and gratitude as I do to you? You have always been by my side.

Mike, Christina, and Mark—Thank you for all the months you endured listening to me talk about this book. Your support and enthusiasm helped me through. You are forever my "kids"!

Grandpa Anatoliy—Your life has been an example to me since I was a child. Only now do I understand the strength of your integrity and character.

Stan Belyshev—Thank you for never withholding correction. You have taught me one of life's most important lessons- having a teachable spirit.

Ksenia Luzanov—Thank you for all the hours you took to edit this book. You've made me a better writer.

Teddy Dobek—Thanks for the great graphic contribution to the cover!

Alex Verbetsky—Thank you for the photography.

Endorsements

The Standard Christian Epidemic is an honest approach to addressing the problem of being followers of man rather than being disciples of Christ. God never intended for His people to center their life around what man has experienced but rather what Christ has said and made available to His disciples. We live in a church culture which Paul described as "changing the glory of the incorruptible God into an image made like corruptible man..." (Romans 1:23). No wonder we are not seeing the supernatural results Christ promised. We can't have that glory when we model life after another man. Jesus said, "He that believes in Me, the works that I do he will do also; and greater works than these he will do, because I go unto My Father" (John 14:12). The key is having faith in Christ and following His ways.

David does a great, to the point, job on addressing these issues. How many people have wasted their lives trying to live in a box that man created when God desired them to do so much more. If God needed another John Wesley, Smith Wigglesworth, or Kathryn Kuhlman, He could have. But, God chose you to be *you*. God doesn't want copies of another believer, He wants you to be open to His move, and true to the authentic identity He gave you. The thing I love most about this book is that it exposes the lie that we are cookie cutter molds of God, and gives us permission to let the life of Christ manifest through us just the way God designed.

Hear the words of this book calling us to authenticity in our relationship with God. Read it slowly, meditatively, waiting for these truths to become revelation to you personally. There is no doubt that David has heard from God. Your walk with Christ will see new horizons by heeding the words God gave to this man under the inspiration of

His Holy Spirit. The standard is being raised, and this is the call of God: to break free from the Standard Christian Epidemic.

Mark Casto
Pastor, Omega Center International

David's writing stirred me and reminded me of my obligation to continually refresh my relationship with the Father. No matter how mature you find yourself, whether as little children, young men or as fathers (1 John 2:12-14) this book will edify, exhort, and comfort you as you overcome all things in fulfilling your calling and election. I can wholeheartedly recommend this book to every one of God's children.

Carroll Sanders
Minister, Lighthouse Christian Center

David's new book provides rich, powerful encouragement for every Christian fighting for spiritual survival, and that would include most of us at some point. But more than that, David is pointing the way for the next generation, the up and coming generation that so desperately needs to know truth and the hope that we have in Christ. There is only One in whom we will find truth, as David relays in this book clearly, Jesus Christ our Lord Savior.

Gail Manizak
Founder/CEO, The Power and Presence Ministry

The body of Christ must rise up to the maturity that it has been called to walk in, and this is only possible by the Spirit of God who dwells within the Christian. This book addresses the problem of Christians who are walking by what others are doing instead of what the Spirit of God is doing. The Holy Spirit only does what the Father and the Son are doing; this is a revelation that Christians must receive to fulfill their true calling and mandate. This book goes into detail to describe how Christians should desire to walk with the Lord each and everyday, in the Victory Jesus Christ died to give us.

Adam Larson
Founder, Ministering Spirits Ministries

David has a diligent thirst to know, understand, and live in the fullness of all God has promised. He remains a student of the Holy Spirit, ever in search of more revelation unfolding through uncountable hours of study in scripture. God has reached down and plucked him, gave Him the mind of Christ so that he may be a vessel of use by the Almighty.

The words within this book stress the importance of being and living a spirit filled life through the Lord's Comforter, the Holy Ghost. It is through the Spirit of God that scripture is no longer text but experience, the actual discovery of one's final identity, purpose, and path.

Lenora Sarver
CEO, Prophetic Intuition Ministry

Contents

Foreword

We are living in wonderful days when God is moving in the earth as never before. One of the most exciting elements of this present move of God is the way that the Holy Spirit is touching young men and women, enabling them to lead and inspire their generation to walk in the fullness of God. David Vilkhovoy is one such young man. I have known him for some time and have remarked upon both his hunger and maturity in the things of the Kingdom of God.

It is my joy and pleasure to commend to you David's new book. In the Standard Christian Epidemic, David explores in depth the theme of calling the church back to the standard of Jesus Christ instead of that of religion and reliance on self which has hindered the church for so long.

Drawing on scripture and personal experience, David takes the reader on a journey away from the fickle sands of basing one's Christian life on sense knowledge alone and challenges us to live by every word that proceeds from the mouth of God. David encourages his reader to dig the wells of intimacy with God and to learn the disciplines of living and ministering from the Secret Place.

The Standard Christian Epidemic will enable you to grow in your faith and equip you to develop a lifestyle as a part of a new Joshua generation. A believer who can fully enter into God's land of exceedingly great and precious promises by which we are made partakers of God's divine nature (2 Peter 1:2-4).

I heartily recommend this book to you and believe you will be blessed by it.

Rev. Graham Jones
International Gospel Outreach

Introduction

The idea of the Standard Christian Epidemic was birthed through various trials of my life in which I questioned God and His work among His people. I knew one thing to be true- God is God. If God is God, He is good, righteous and perfect. There it is. He is perfect. Take a moment and think about that. *He is perfect.*

This was a fundamental groundbreaker for me. If God was perfect, I asked myself, why do so many Christians fail in their walks with God? Why do so many Christians struggle in their personal and spiritual lives? So many Christians today are just a resemblance of society, a beaten world. This is where the Lord began to reveal the message of this book to me. It occurred as I was writing one of my first sermons for my youth group. I don't remember how these words came into my mind but I never forgot them. *The Standard Christian Epidemic.*

That is the concept of this book. It was clear to me that the Lord wanted to expose this hypocritical Christian way of life. In the context of this message, I am defining "epidemic" as a false widespread belief. The epidemic here is in the widespread belief of the "standard Christian," a Christian that lives life based on the experience of others. They label other Christians as the standard for their own Christian lifestyle. For example, if they see a Christian struggling with their finances, they may accept that as a standard for their own life. As Christians we don't intentionally do this, but this action is almost committed subconsciously. Instead of looking to our standard, Jesus Christ, we look at other Christians, which contradicts the whole basis of Christianity, to be "Christ-like." Do you see how much trouble you can get into by following other Christians and building your experiences around them? You will not succeed in your walk with

God if you continue to live in this manner because the One who made you is Jesus Christ and you were made in His Image; not in the image of man. Every man is corrupt and a liar, but there is One who is true; His name is Jesus Christ.

This is my desire for Christians worldwide, to fall in love with Jesus Christ and follow Him wholeheartedly, not looking to the right or left, but keeping their eyes steadfast upon Him who loved us first.

Chapter 1
Experiencing God

There is a powerful book written by Henry Blackaby in which he makes a practical case on how to experience God. He highlights powerful truths that show the reality of God and why we may or may not see Him at work in our lives. Much of my revelation and fundamental experience came from that book. Blackaby builds an entire case for knowing and doing the will of God, which I strongly recommend to every Christian. In this book however, I am only going to touch upon it as it relates to the standard Christian.

A standard Christian is one who uses other Christians as his or her standard. When this is done, there is no room for God to work. We limit God when we expect Him to do only what we have seen done in others' lives, but God works when we realize He is God and able to do anything. Yes, we are called to co-labor with Him and follow His dictates, but behind the scenes He is the one moving the mountains. You speak and do, but it is He who actually *does*. It is according to His power in us that we are able to move mountains and cast down strongholds.

That you may know... what is the exceeding greatness of His power toward us who believe, according to the working of His mighty power which He worked in Christ when He raised Him from the dead and seated Him at His right hand in the heavenly places. (Ephesians 1:18-20)

The "exceeding greatness of His power" declares the truth that it is God's power and nothing of our own strength. The next line "toward us who believe," is speaking of you and me; that we have the potential to experience His power in our lives. When we realize that He is the one behind it all, we start to solely rely on Him. We no longer depend on man's strength, nor do we look at what others are experiencing, because we realize God is God alone. Until we let go of our own might, we will not see His might. When you rely only on yourself to do something, very little will come of it. But when you trust an almighty God, nothing is impossible. So the question to ask here is, how can you expect to experience God if you don't start depending completely on Him?

I believe God deals with us on an individual basis. Each person has a measure of experience. The person who will experience God the most is the one who opens his bosom to the Spirit of God. The measure you give is the measure you will receive (Luke 6:38). I am talking about *faith capacity*. The capacity of faith you have towards God is the amount of belief you have towards God. Jesus said, **"Let it be done according to your faith"** (Matt. 9:29; Matt. 15:28). In other words, He can only do for you what you believe. You must understand that there is always more room in your heart for God. *Always.* God knows it and you know it. God waits for those decisions of our hearts.

Your ego is the part of your heart that doesn't belong to God. It is that place that tries to get "you" back on the throne. It is in fact a stronghold of pride. So when we come before God in our quiet times, we need to continually open ourselves up and let the Holy Spirit take those things captive. When we willingly give Him reign, He grabs a firm hold and we release the power and authority of Jesus Christ into our lives. This is a promise from God.

> *Casting down arguments and every high thing that exalts itself against the knowledge of God, bringing every thought into captivity to the obedience of Christ.* (2 Corinthians 10:5)

This however is not quickly done; it is done in solitude with God. Your soul is unsearchable, but your spirit, quickened by the Holy Spirit, knows the depths of your soul. Therefore, when you unite with the Holy Spirit through your spirit, you begin to give reign to Jesus Christ over every thought of disobedience and over *every high thing that exalts itself against the knowledge of God.*

The Apostle Paul said, "Work out your salvation" (Philippians 2:12), which is a reference to renewing your mind and living from the Presence of God, rather than living by vain imagination, which we hold until we surrender to Jesus Christ. Here are a couple passages that speak on our spirit man having that access to our soul when quickened by the Holy Spirit.

> *The spirit of a man is the lamp of the Lord, searching all the inner depths of his heart.* (Proverbs 20:27)

> *But there is a spirit in man, and the breath of the Almighty gives him understanding.* (Job 32:8)

We see two things here. It is with the Holy Spirit that we are able to get understanding of our soul. Second, when we acquire that understanding, we are able to surrender it to Christ. And so it is in this place where we enlarge our capacity to trust God. God simply cannot move in your life unless you trust Him. You may ask "Why is that so?", and the truth is that our authority releases His Power. God is limited to our choice. It goes back to Adam and Eve when God gave Adam authority over all the earth (Genesis 1:26). From that point on, man was given a free will to choose, as he would please. To this day, we still have a choice to do as we please. It is not God to invade your free will. Your free will is a gift from God. He gave us a choice, because he is not interested in passive love; rather, He created us to freely fellowship with Him, wholeheartedly submitted.

To have effective faith means to actively trust God. When we accept Jesus Christ as Lord, we are born-again; our spirits made new. Though we are made new, we still have to sanctify ourselves by allowing the Holy Spirit to renew our minds through His Word. Accepting Jesus is only the beginning. There is a process of refinement afterwards. Your free will has to be constantly exercised to bring God into every aspect of your life. You will always have choices to make. Even though you are born-again and made new, you can still make decisions that won't reflect your born-again self. It is in our hands to continue to accept His grace. That's why we can still miss it in areas of our lives where we know God should have His place. For example, some of us constantly get sick. This is not the will of God. Jesus commanded us to pray, "Let it be on earth as it is in heaven." Heaven does not have any sick people. But we continue to be sick because a renewal of the mind has not fully occurred. The Word of God has to become a stronghold in your life before it can be effective. *For by Grace you were saved, continue therefore in the same manner... work out your salvation* (Ephesians 2:8; Philippians 2:12).

Your free will can be the best and worst part of you. One can stop the *exceeding greatness* of God in their life and at the same time be a co-heir with Christ. We may confess Jesus as Lord and savior, but we must also walk according to His Word. God will not invade our lives without our consent. You will not experience God's work in fullness until you surrender.

It's like holding a cup. The cup represents your life. You are clutching this cup with your hand, refusing anyone else to hold it. In ignorance, you act self-righteous and trust only yourself with it. In reality, you don't know how to handle it, but you still clutch it, fearing you will lose it. But as you begin to release it the tension breaks and you begin to feel freedom. Then as you finally let go and say, "Yes, Jesus, take my life, take all of me," a miracle begins to occur. Your life begins to turn around and a situation that had no end in sight begins to turn in your favor. You gain peace and purpose; content that God now has your life. This all happens because the Lord Jesus is now in charge of your life.

Don't clutch your life out of fear of losing it. You will never lose anything you surrender to Jesus. He simply begins to take care of it.

For whoever desires to save his life will lose it, but whoever loses his life for My sake will find it. (Matthew 16:25)

†

Chapter 2
Holy Spirit Led

A mistake many "experienced" Christians make is forgetting that the director is the Holy Spirit. In my life, I pray for people that are close to me especially if I know they are struggling in life. However, I will also pray for friends and family that I know are not experiencing God's best. As Christians we should keep one another in constant reminder, observing one another's fruit, so that we can challenge one another to strive for God's best.

However there was a time that I was misled in praying for others. We all have moments in life where we get caught up in the emotion of what we are praying for. By this, I mean that we disregard any other prayer and focus on that one prayer. From personal experience, I found myself walking into prayer, praying for that one issue, and walking out still praying for it. It came to a point where I began to feel like I was alone in prayer, the Holy Spirit absent. Throughout this time, I began to ask myself, "Why isn't the Holy Spirit telling me what to pray for anymore?" As I asked myself this question and observed my life from the side, I began to see that I had completely ignored the Holy Spirit in my prayers. I had begun praying only for what I thought I should pray for. By doing this, I neglected the prayers that might have had the most impact.

When one takes God out of the picture, it doesn't matter how sincere they are in prayer; God becomes absent to them. He never leaves us, but we can ignore Him, making His presence of no effect. We can also make the Word of God ineffectual in our lives if we don't abide by it (Mark 7:13). It dawned upon me that I had been missing the point. I began to see that I needed to let go of all prayers and simply come back to Jesus. I began to realize that *my* burdens would go nowhere because the fight was not led by the Holy Spirit.

Yes, the Holy Spirit wants us to have victory in our fights, but if He is not there, we are powerless against any foe. This truth was affirmed to me by prophecy when a well-known prophet had visited our local church with his staff. As we lined up to receive personal prayer and prophecy, I had no special request other than receiving prayer. To my surprise, as one of the staff was praying, out of the blue she began to say, "You are praying for something, stop praying, this is not your burden. When you step over it, then I can move and My Spirit will touch it." Along with other things that were said, God clearly spoke to me to stop praying in this manner. He was speaking specifically to the matter on hand. This will happen with any prayer in your life, when you keep going at it on your own, whether it be intercessory prayer or petitionary prayer. He led me to the realization that in any matter, He is the one doing the work and I must simply cooperate with Him to see the results.

In "Experiencing God", Henry Blackaby outlines seven realities of God; one of those realities is that God is the mastermind behind all things, so it is futile to do things without Him.

> *"For my thoughts are not your thoughts. Nor are your ways My ways," says the Lord.* (Isaiah 55:8)

You will never comprehend His omnipotence. Rather, you must be attentive to what He is doing in your life so that you can join Him and bring it into manifestation. I came to another wonderful conclusion through all this. God *wants* to change my situations. In the past, I would subconsciously accept my circumstances as "the way it is," like most of us do, but God showed me that He wanted to raise me to new heights. In "No High Like the Most High," Kent Mattox writes, "No matter how high you have already gone or how low you have fallen, He has a plan for you that is greater than anything you could have ever imagined." But if we attempt to do it without the Holy Spirit, it will come to nothing. We must seek God and be patient; He will reveal His work. You can then move forward as you sense Him leading. This will bring a prosperous result, because you are joining God.

It is important to remember that God is always at work around you, but His manifestation depends on your cooperation. The phrase "God is always at work" means God's word and power is readily available and His strategies are already set in place. You will read more about this principle in Chapter 4, but having understood this, we must realize it is useless for us to pray if God is not leading us in it. Prayer is necessary in all aspects, but when you come to a certain stature in God, you begin to realize how much more He needs you to be directed by Him. After all, He is the Master. His way is the *only* way that will bring a prosperous result.

> So shall My word be that goes forth from My mouth; It shall not return to Me void, but it shall accomplish what I please, and it shall prosper **in the thing** for which I sent it. (Isaiah 55:11)

I cannot stress the importance of being led by the Holy Spirit in your prayers. Let the Holy Spirit lead you in who to pray for and what to pray for. Yes, you can pray for those on your mind and heart (many times it is already the Holy Spirit leading you), but let the Spirit be your ultimate guide. When you pray as the Holy Spirit leads you, you will have more confidence in your prayers. It is easier to trust God than yourself, when we take Him at His word. If He said, "My Word never returns void *in the thing* I send it for," then we can trust *His* prayers will bring a prosperous result.

Your prayers will begin to unite heaven and earth. If you can imagine that revelation for a moment, your life will be revolutionized. All God wants is for us to bring heaven to earth, making all things new, bringing Him all the glory (Matthew 6:10). Heaven is beauty in all its glory. Some people hold on to the earth only because they haven't glimpsed the reality of heaven. I promise you, as you draw near to God, all heaven will draw near to you! You will see heaven with your spirit.

Just as you can see Jesus in your spirit, you can also see heaven. Hold fast to Him and He will manifest Himself to you.

> *And he who loves Me will be loved by My Father, and I will love him and manifest Myself to him.* (James 4:8)

Chapter 3
Disclaimer

There are many good things you can share with others, but disclosure to the wrong people can have negative consequences. In your perspective, your *treasure* may lose its value, but this is not the case. It's not that your treasure has lost its value; it just went to the wrong place. You will have to uproot those seeds that are planted from *throwing pearl to swine*.

> *Do not give what is holy to the dogs; nor cast your pearls before swine, lest they trample them under their feet, and turn and tear you in pieces.* (Matthew 7:6)

There is much that God reveals to us, which is not necessarily to share with others. He is doing a work in you that no man can see. He is an invisible God and is found in the Secret Place. No one can see what is going on inside your heart. So if you begin to open the treasures of your heart to people, many will not understand you. The work God is doing is invisible to them. And as scripture says, God works in mysterious ways: *My thoughts are not your thoughts and My ways are not your ways* (Isaiah 55:8). Be mindful and careful when sharing your heart with others. It is exciting and tends to be hard to hold back, but you will learn it is much better to only release that which God allows you to release. He knows that if you open yourself up to certain people, you will feel like you lost something. Some revelations apply only to your heart at that time. That is my disclaimer for the message contained in this book.

College Majors

As it relates to work, I am perplexed at the number of Christians around me showing concern for the job market. It is as if this carnal attitude has to exist in the confines of our lives. There is no faith found in the words, "I hope the job market gets better when I graduate," or questions such as, "Does this industry have enough demand for my major?" When we begin to question our career paths and choices based on a carnal mentality, we have lost all sight of God. God does not merely exist in your "prayer closet," but He exists in every part of your life. *In all your ways, acknowledge Him and He shall direct your paths.* (Proverbs 3:6). Your job opportunity does not lie in how good the job market is. It is wise to plan and see what options are better, but it is another matter when we base our decisions on what we see rather than what we believe God has spoken. If you feel led by God into a certain career, but because of poor job prospects you change direction, you are operating out of a carnal mind.

I continue to be frustrated with Christians that have demoted God to a man; God is not a man. Therefore, do not run around like the pagans do trying to find the "right" fit into the marketplace. Commit your ways to God and *He will direct your paths* (Proverbs 3:6). If you feel led to go into a certain major, then do it. Don't listen to your aunt pestering you about what you are studying and going off about a bad job market. Did God not lead you into this major? Will you choose to believe what a man will tell you? Will you allow doubt to creep upon you like a fog, blurring your vision? *Do not trust man, who has but a breath in his nostrils, of what account is he* (Isaiah 2:22). But rather as Jesus said, *man does not live on bread alone, but by every word that proceeds out of the mouth of God* (Matthew 4:4). I have wondered many times about my own career path, debating the right choice. Little did I realize I was actually fighting God. Thankfully, God would not budge from His divine plan for my life.

When starting my college career at a community college, I was relieved to know I did not have to choose a specific component of business until I transferred to a four-year university. From the start of my community college to the end of it, I was set on studying management. Upon entering the University of Massachusetts in the fall of 2009, I began to consider a different component of business: finance. During the course of my time at the community college and the quickly forgotten summer, I bought into the words people spoke and allowed confusion to build. People began to tell me that a finance degree would put me in a much better position for a job, so after much thought I hesitantly decided to declare my major in finance. I studied one year as a finance major, but each semester got progressively worse. At my second semester, I could no longer hide the pressure within my heart to switch back to management. Truth be told, job prospects are a lot worse for management majors, but my heart knew what it desired and what God had spoken. He gave me this desire and I finally understood after a three-year battle that whatever choice God lays upon your heart is always the best choice.

I contacted my advisor and told him of my decision to switch majors; soon after, I was a declared management major. As soon as I switched to management, I felt a pressure release and regained a sense of direction. I knew I had finally chosen God in this matter. By then I was a senior and it was my first semester taking management courses. I never felt more satisfaction in my college career than I did that final year. I was able to learn and understand the course material with enthusiasm, as much as is possible in school. I also grew in courage and confidence by having to do a lot of public speaking. Group projects and presentations forced me to work in teams, which was something I never liked. I did not enjoy group work because of the many pointless meetings that take place. But I felt the Lord's humorous smile on me when I sat through those meetings, because we both knew it was a lesson I had to learn. I began to see the Lord was teaching me to accept teamwork, because groups of people can do a lot more than individuals alone. All along, God knew what was best for me. This decision taught me the bottom line: God's decision for us will stand through time and we will know His choice. In retrospect, don't listen to your aunts and grandmothers when it comes to already knowing what God has spoken to you. Yes, we should seek counsel from trusted people in our lives, but your final decision needs to be in faith of what you believe God has spoken to you.

Learn to Know the Witness

Another secret we must attain is to learn to know the Witness. The Witness is the Holy Spirit. God speaks to you through the Holy Spirit. It is He who stands as a witness, confirming that you are indeed a child of God (Romans 8:16). In your walk with Him, practice evaluating His voice. Evaluate what you hear, so that you can prove whether it is from God or not. You can do this by examining what you believe He is speaking to you when trying to make a decision. Make the decisions always in faith of what you believe He is speaking to you. Don't be afraid to admit the times you may have mistaken God's voice with your own. By being honest with yourself, you will learn to be more sensitive to His voice and know when He is speaking. God will fix our mistakes and continue with His plan even when we stumble, but practice going back to your decisions and evaluating whether what you heard was from God. Assess what you felt in your heart at the time and what choice you actually made. Now that you know the outcome of the matter, examine whether it was the right choice. It is okay to have missed it; we all do and will. But the more we practice this, the more we will learn to know the Witness. And we will be able to make the best decisions every time.

The Witness is always confirmed. The Witness will confirm Himself. Your heart will confirm the Witness. Other people will confirm the Witness. But learn to know the Witness. Through experience, you will learn to know His voice.

My sheep hear My voice, and I know them, and they follow Me.
(John 10:27)

✝

Chapter 4
Doing What the Father is Doing

Jesus said, "I say what I hear the Father saying. I do what I see the Father doing. I do nothing of Myself. *My Father has been working to this day as I am working*" (John 5:17). As in Jesus' life, the Father is always doing something in your life. He gives you His ideas and innovations. He is always speaking something to you that you must be releasing. He is actively working in your life, but whether it manifests or not is up to you. For example, as a youth group minister, I am responsible to initiate that which God is already doing. He is healing every ache, forgiving every sin, accepting and comforting the broken hearted; He is speaking words of knowledge and wisdom to those that need direction and guidance. He is delivering all who are oppressed. But we must understand that the manifestation is not contingent upon God's actions, but upon ours. If I as a youth leader am not attentive to God, then He will not be able to work through me. If God lays it upon my heart to call someone out with migraine headaches, but I ignore that directive, then His will to heal that individual will not come to pass at that time. Now, if we are obedient to His voice, then we will see manifestations take place. Miracles, healings, and freedoms await those who are willing to step out in faith and exercise their God-given authority.

It is imperative to note a certain truth. God is so in love with us that He does all He can for us, even changing us, when we are completely ignorant of Him. I began to understand this when in my spirit I saw a spinning whirlwind in the area of my belly. This was an image in my "mind's eye," as the world calls it. It is also known as "seeing with your heart," while this is in fact "seeing with your spirit". We often hear such clichés, because the world does not actually understand what this is. Christians should have greater intuition and understanding because our spirits are united with God, but it is tuning into our spirit that we need to work on. When God says, "Draw near to Me and I will draw near to you," He is doing us a favor; it is our connection to Him that gives us the supernatural ability to see and hear what is uncommon to the natural man.

I saw this powerful whirlwind circling at lightning speed, round and round, and I heard the words, "I am always working in you, changing you into the image of My Son." When we commit our lives to God, He begins to mold us into the image of His Son. However, the extent to which we open up is the extent to which He can work in us. Nevertheless, God is always at work, molding us into the image of Christ. When we are faithless, He remains faithful (2 Timothy 2:13), meaning He is a Father that never turns His back on His children.

However, I am not at all implying that we will be changed if we remain passive. His work in us accelerates at the pace our faith grows. His faithfulness does not give us an excuse to "slack off." Rather, His faithfulness motivates us to move forward even stronger. One may begin to question how then does God carry out His will if we don't respond. Be not deceived, God is not handicapped without us. His will shall come to pass, but through others. The question is whether you will be a part of it.

His purposes have been fulfilled throughout history: the creation, the preparation for the coming of Jesus, the hundreds of prophecies, the preparation of the Bible, a manuscript that has maintained its original content in far more copies than any other book in history, and the decades of the various movements of the body of Christ through the five-fold ministries, in which God was establishing His church. What God wills, He fulfills. But in your personal life, what God wills only comes to pass if *you* also will.

Before I get into the details of God's work in my own life, I want to unveil the ultimate example, Jesus Christ, who fulfilled God's will to the fullest. In every point He was tempted as we are (Hebrews 4:15), but He trusted God and overcame. Not only did He fulfill the perfect will of God in His personal life, but also accomplished the greatest task in history. He came from heaven to defeat that, which was corrupt. His assignment was to crucify the flesh so that man no longer carried corruption. As Jesus hung on the cross dying, He cried out, "It is finished" (John 19:30). He ended the reign of sin. Fear no longer had authority over man if He chose Christ's atonement. Man was now free from the law of sin and death (Romans 8:2).

Study the scriptures and you will see the beautiful story God painted for us. His son Jesus was the firstborn of many sons and daughters to come.

> *For whom He foreknew, He also predestined to be conformed to the image of His son, so that He might be the firstborn among many brethren.* (Romans 8:29)

Jesus is our big Brother. In every way, He is our role model. The common misconception in standard Christianity is the logic that Jesus was only God, therefore we cannot necessarily relate to Him. That is an extremely wrong ideology. Jesus served as the purest and most complete example for us to follow. He lived from the very conception of life to the final breath on the cross in the perfect Will of God. He had to walk through the same trials and be tested in the same way we are tested. He had no special powers to overcome sin, but the Spirit of God that we all possess. He was like you and I in every respect, otherwise He would not be found qualified to serve as the High Priest. While He was on earth, Jesus did all that He saw the Father doing, healing and restoring people. The Father was also delivering legions of demons. The Father was comforting prostitutes and sinners. He showed compassion to the children, "the least of them" (Matthew 25:40).

But over all, the Father was breaking the power of sin in every individual's life. The Father did all those things while Jesus walked the earth. Jesus saw the Father's work and partnering with Him, brought it into manifestation. Jesus spoke when He heard the Father say,

"Lazarus come forth," and when He commanded the winds at storm to cease. He healed when He saw the Father healing. Jesus revealed the Father's compassion. More than anything else, Jesus portrayed what the Father was like. It saddens me when I hear people blaming God for the disasters and woes of the world. My friends, did Jesus cause anyone to become sick while He was on earth? We would never claim nor say such things about Jesus, but we do about God. I want to show you a beautiful secret to end such religious talks.

> *Being justified freely by His grace through the redemption that is in Christ Jesus, whom God set forth as a* **propitiation** *by His blood, through faith, to demonstrate His righteousness, because in His forbearance God had passed over the sins that were previously committed, to demonstrate at the present time His righteousness, that He might be just and the justifier of the one who has faith in Jesus.* (Romans 3:24-26)

> *Yet it* **pleased** *the Lord to bruise Him; He has put Him to grief.* (Isaiah 53:10)

In the first passage, it is written that the blood of Jesus Christ was the appeasement for our sins. Along with the second passage, this implies that Jesus satisfied the wrath of God for all the sin that was committed and is to be committed. As Andrew Wommack put it, man is no longer judged based on his sin, but based on whether he accepts Jesus Christ (John 16:9). Furthermore, God is not judging people right now. There will come a Day of Judgment, but to say God causes the evil in our world contradicts the very Word of God.

Some people don't understand how it could please God to bruise Jesus (Isaiah 53:10), but remember that Jesus was slain from the foundation of the world (Revelation 13:8). God the Father, Jesus Christ, and the Holy Spirit knew man would fall and would be in need of redemption. Jesus willingly went to earth to appease the wrath of sin. It was not only God the Father who desired justification, but Jesus the Word of God. The Bible says it pleased God to bruise Him, but it is in fact a mutual satisfaction between Christ and the Father.

God being a just and holy judge could not allow sin to go unpunished. In today's world, a good judge would never allow evil to go unpunished. God is so much more than a good judge; He is a perfect judge. He is incredibly wise, magnificent, and entirely perfect. It is difficult to write about His justice, because there are no words to describe how terribly glorious He is. When sin was committed, it was an unruly evil in the sight of God. It had to be made right. It was the unfathomable love of God that caused Jesus to come to earth. God Himself stepped down from His throne to fix man's mistake. What He had no part in, He took completely upon Himself. In all this, it is of utmost importance to realize that Jesus was and is the face of God the Father. All that Jesus did portrayed the image and nature of God. He alone is the perfect representation of God, for who else has come down from heaven but the Son of God to know and reveal these things (John 3:13)? Jesus affirmed this truth to the disciple Philip who did not realize that Jesus and the Father were one.

> *Philip said to Him, "Lord, show us the Father, and it is sufficient for us." Jesus said to him, "Have I been with you so long, and yet you have not known Me, Philip? He who has seen Me has seen the Father; so how can you say, 'Show us the Father'?* [10] *Do you not believe that I am in the Father, and the Father in Me?*
> (John 14:8-10)

This all goes back to the fact that we need to live as Jesus lived, in unison with the Father. Once we accept that Jesus is our example in all that we do, we can examine our own lives in comparison to Him. We cannot find any viable excuse to not be more like Him. As we begin to follow God in every area of our lives, we will see His manifestation. He will reveal His work to us and we will be able to join Him in it. Even today, God is revealing things to you that you must be doing. The question remains: are you fulfilling all that the Father is doing in your life? Are you aware of His work? Many of us have denied the omnipotence of God because we trust Him so little. We treat God as if He's like any other human; We think He cannot fix our problems, therefore we never see the problem go away. To allow God to be effective in your life, you must actively trust Him.

During the days of this revelation, I began to feel a heaviness coming in my spirit and as I was in prayer one day, the heaviness began to increase. An uncontrollable lament of the heart came over me as I began to repeat over and over again, "Holy Spirit forgive me for treating you like a man." I realized I had not trusted Him. The Lord was prophesying to me. He began to reveal how hurt He had been because of my lack of trust.

There come moments when we feel comfortable to take the reins of our lives, but it is then that we lose sight of God. However we acknowledge who is in charge when trouble comes around the corner. We begin to see how helpless and hopeless we are. God never desires to leave us alone, but if we let go of Him, being a gentleman He has no choice but to step back. Don't allow self-righteousness to rule you, because it only wants to destroy you. Evaluate your life. How much do you actually trust God? The truth is that God will not be mocked; what a man sows, he will reap (Galatians 6:7). If you build your relationship based on trust, you will surely experience Him in your life, but if you continue to ignore His reality, even the knowledge that you have will be taken away from you (Matthew 13:12), for the secrets of the Lord belong to His people (Psalm 25:14).

Today, silence your heart before Him; bow before Him in humility. Assess how much value and recognition you give Him. Have you looked past His power and ability? Think of all the times you were confused and did not trust God to take care of you. Ask the Holy Spirit for forgiveness. It's not your repentance He demands, but your trust. We acknowledge our trust and helplessness when we repent. You must actively believe that He is your provider. Otherwise, He is limited to your faith.

> For he who comes to God must believe that He is, and that He is
> a rewarder of those who diligently seek Him. (Hebrews 11:6)

God has no problem taking care of us. He is fully capable of dealing with any problem, but He needs our submission. He works based on our faith in Him. He does not move where He is not accepted. If you choose not to believe, you can live your whole life without seeing the evidence of God. He does not manifest Himself to the world, only to those that love Him.

> "He who has My commandments and keeps them, it is he who
> loves Me. And he who loves Me will be loved by My Father, and
> I will love him and manifest Myself to him."

Judas (not Iscariot) said to Him, "Lord, how is it that You will manifest Yourself to us, and not to the world?"

Jesus answered and said to him, "If anyone loves Me, he will keep My word; and My Father will love him, and We will come to him and make Our home with him. (John 14:21-23)

Relationship with God

Your relationship with God, like any other relationship, is not a roller coaster. As Andrew Wommack put it, "Relationship is not sustained by intensity." We need to practice coming before God in simple faith. It should not be based on any emotions, good or bad. In whatever state you are in, come before Him with praise and thanksgiving; develop that relationship with Him. Even in your temptations, come to Him. I've had times of temptation where I would come before the Lord, telling Him how I was feeling. Instead of feeling His distance, I felt Him even closer as His arms wrapped around me. He is not there to point a finger at you. He desires a love relationship, and He always has.

Recall the story of Jesus and the adulteress. A woman was brought before Jesus, condemned by the crowd for her act. They tested Jesus by asking Him what should be done because the law demanded her death. In response, Jesus said:

"He who is without sin among you, let him throw a stone at her first" ... Then those who heard it, being convicted by their conscience, went out one by one. And Jesus was left alone, and the woman standing in the midst ... He said to her, "Woman where are those accusers of yours? Has no one condemned you?" She said, "No one, Lord."

And Jesus said to her, "Neither do I condemn you; go and sin no more." (John 8:7-11)

Whether we sin or not, Jesus doesn't accuse us. On the contrary, it is He who pardons our guilt. It is a crime against the blood of Jesus to feel guilty once we have already accepted His redemption. Come before God in your good and bad. We're not always going to be perfect, but if we keep coming back to Him, He remains faithful to us.

We should also be mindful not to base our current relationship with God on our past experiences. Whatever you have experienced in the past, God calls you to move forward with Him in a new way. Friends don't sit and talk about what they did the week before; rather, they seek new experiences. Any good relationship is progressive and does not live in the past. Past experiences create testimonies and stakes in the Lord, but they do not dictate today's agenda. If we rely on our past experiences, we are placing limitations on the new things God has in store for us. We are limited beings that can only move and see in one direction. God can see and move in many directions. Never label one direction as God's because He will reappear somewhere else and you won't recognize that. His numerous thoughts and ways are as far above us as the heavens are from the earth (Isaiah 55:9). He will hold your hand throughout life and lead you through all things. He knows exactly where He is leading you and His grace will follow you all the days of your life. Hold onto His hand, because He will never let go.

Chapter 5
The Standard Christian Epidemic

In this chapter, I want to illustrate the life of Jesus Christ and the example He sets for us. I also want to reveal how we are to follow His example in all that we do, as opposed to looking at other Christians.

> *We must always keep in mind that it is all about Jesus Christ.*
> (Colossians 1:17)

Just as in Paul's time, Christians are drawn to each other (1 Corinthians 1:12-13). It is human tendency to cling to another person, but God wants us to cling to Him. Man will fail, but God will not fail. He calls us to focus on Him at all times, for His Word will never waver, but many in the Christian world live their lives based on what they see others experiencing. This is a dangerous slope for the Christian.

The error lies in this: we claim Jesus as God, but accept other Christians' experiences as "the way it is." Who has deceived you into such thinking? There is no greater crime against Christianity than to label it by any other name than the name of Jesus Christ. He said, "I am the way, the truth, and the life" (John 14:6). The *standard Christian epidemic* is Christians relating to one another through their victories and defeats. For example, you can look at me today, teaching the Word of God, and be affirmed in the truth of the Gospel; but if the following year my life goes downhill, and you are discouraged in your own faith, then you are misled. You cannot build your altar on anyone but Jesus.

He is your sacrifice and He is the one found worthy to be your ransom. It is He that was qualified to die for you, not me or anyone else.

Jesus never expected us to walk the Christian life relying on other Christians. Jesus Christ is Christianity. There is no mention in the Word of God about *trusting* other Christians and their experiences. Nowhere does God tell us to get through life by holding onto one another. *Trust in the Lord with all your heart and lean not on your own understanding* (Proverbs 3:5). The verse refers not only to your understanding but to every other man's too. The answer is simple: Jesus is the only one who conquered the world, and He lives today making intercession on our behalf (Romans 8:34). If you don't make Jesus the focal point of your life, your Christianity will suffer. There is no Christianity without Christ. He has to stay the main point. It is only when you begin to look to the right and left that you begin to stumble in your walk with God, but if you keep your eyes steadfast upon Him, you will *walk on water* as Peter did (Matthew 14:29).

Judging One Another

Just as we cannot look to one another as final examples, we also cannot judge one another. God has perfect standards, so only He can judge. Humans on the other hand have no perfect standard, yet they judge, gossip, and condemn. If Almighty God in all His perfection does not judge us, then how can we judge? Where is the justification in judging your brother or sister when God so freely forgave you? It is an unacceptable lifestyle for the Christian, and inconsistent with the Word of God.

Several years back, I was doing some business online. In one transaction, I was sent the wrong item. I was immediately irritated and pride got the best of me. I was justifying my reaction by saying, "Business is business and it must be done right." I began to write an e-mail in response, demanding I get a discount on the new order, but then I remembered the story of David and the Prophet Nathan. In 2 Samuel 12, the prophet confronts David about his adulterous affair with Bathsheba. He presents King David with a story, similar to King David's own act of sin. Nathan asks David how to act with such a man who dealt wrongly in the situation presented. David responded with harsh judgment, declaring that this man must pay and die! By doing this, King David sentenced his own judgment. The Lord spoke through the prophet, saying "By the mercy you have dealt, I will deal with you" (2 Samuel 12). David realized his sin and repented, coming right with the Lord, but the illegitimate son he conceived with Bathsheba died.

When I remembered that story, I became frightened. I understood that God was speaking to me concerning my mercy. It was of vital importance for me to realize how we need to conduct ourselves with others. As the Word of God says, we need to put on love; we need to continually walk in love and mercy, imitating God's character (Ephesians 5:1). It is wrong for our first response to be *justification* rather than forgiveness. It is not our job to judge people. We are responsible for ourselves; God will take care of the judgment (Proverbs 25:22). There remains no justification in condemnation. This story should show us the backwards way we tend to live, when we believe we are right in judging others. It should be far from us to condemn. Instead, we are to love and forgive on every occasion. God has shown us so much mercy, so let us show it to one another. None of us have any reason to put anyone down for any reason. Because of the grace of God, *there is therefore now no condemnation for those in Christ Jesus* (Romans 8:1). Let us be responsible stewards of this gospel by living it.

Misrepresentation

If not for Jesus Christ, I would have left Christianity a long time ago. There are many Christians that live hypocritical lives and the world mocks Christianity because of it. But to the world I say, let every man fall, but the One who I believe in represents His own name. His name is Jesus Christ. He alone represents Christianity; He shares His glory with no man (Isaiah 42:8). He is the One who saves, preserves and delivers. If someone has wronged you, don't mistake that for Jesus. Your family and friends do not represent Jesus Christ; Jesus represents Himself. Therefore don't allow Satan to deceive you into religion. He will trick you into believing evil acts are of God. He has convinced many that it is God who causes evil in our world. Satan indeed is the father of all lies (John 8:44).

Religion says God punishes us by sending natural disasters or other woes. Religion teaches that God makes us sick to teach us a lesson. Can a kingdom divided against itself stand (Mark 3:24)? Would God use Satan's devices and the very thing that He hates, sin, to discipline the children He loves? Does your natural father call his enemies over to discipline you when you step out of line? Your natural parents would never do such a thing. They would discipline you themselves, because it is their love that will change you. It is so with God; He teaches and matures us through His Word. If we place God somewhere in the middle of using evil, we are denying the truths that Satan is evil and God is good. Our God is an absolute God. His Word makes absolute statements. His Word declares He is a good and loving Father. Study the many names of God to get a better picture of who He really is. If God truly used evil to teach us, then Jesus would have made everyone ill rather than heal all who came to Him: *great multitudes followed Him, and He healed them all* (Matthew 12:15).

Apart from healing, there are natural disasters that people claim are acts of God. Yet natural disasters weren't even brought up in the Bible. The storm at sea that Jesus rebuked was not God trying to kill people; rather it was the natural cycle of the earth. If we assume storms, droughts, hurricanes, etc. are of God, then we are saying that Jesus was trying to kill Himself at sea. One can claim that God initiated the storm so that Jesus could bring glory to Himself by exercising His authority, but even this doesn't line up. Jesus was sound asleep until the disciples woke him up. This was one of those things that just came up and when it did, Jesus exercised His authority. Instead of thanking God for the storm, He turned to His disciples and rebuked their lack of faith. Jesus made no mention of this being a part of God's plan. I am making no claim that it was or wasn't, but I am observing how Jesus looked at it. Jesus rebuked both the storm and his disciples for being afraid. If we claim God sent the storm, why would He rebuke them for it? Christ denied giving any power to that storm, meaning God had no part in it. To Him, it appeared to be a normal everyday thing that He didn't even flinch at. This can lead us to make the assumption that Jesus understood storms came and went and had no God-given agenda to kill people.

When sin entered the world, the earth itself was cursed, no longer being the earth God created it to be (Romans 8:20). Sin became a natural cycle of the earth. Before Adam's sin, creation was lively and vibrant; afterwards, everything was tainted. Sin brought corruption and death. The point I am making is that it is not God who brings chaos to the world. God's kingdom brings order. He commanded us to bring His kingdom to earth. It is our job to represent God as Jesus represented Him: by healing the sick, casting out devils, and preaching the Gospel.

The most important lesson in this chapter is to learn of Jesus Christ. As you do, you will know how to live a successful Christian life that will be followed by signs and wonders. As Christians, we have nothing to fear when we are with Him. Jesus stated, "The ruler of this world is coming, and he has nothing in Me" (John 14:30). We too, as children of God, have no part with Satan. If we continue in Christ, we will become like Him. Satan will not be able to deceive us when we abide in Christ. Though Jesus was tempted with lies from Satan, He was never fooled. Fear not; if we abide in Him, we too won't be fooled.

> *These things I have spoken to you, that in Me you may have peace. In the world you will have tribulation; but be of good cheer, I have overcome the world.* (John 16:33)

Chapter 6
Seasons

In every season of your life, God is at work. Every season has a purpose before God. You will be greatly blessed if you recognize and accept this reality, as it will put your life into perspective; you will begin to realize how to live in every season. The Bible speaks often about it:

> To everything, there is a season, a time for every purpose under heaven... He has made everything beautiful in its time.
>
> (Eccl. 3:1; 11)

What I have seen in my life are the many seasons that pass people by without them ever discerning and living that season's purpose. Many people choose not to accept the responsibility and calling that God has placed on their lives. They believe if they ignore the calling, they waive any personal responsibility. The truth is that if you ignore your calling, you make a conscious decision to do so while others make a conscious decision to accept their calling. Those that understand what God is doing are those that will flourish in every season. They will live content, eager, and expectant of God. It is not a matter of *waiting* for a season, for God has said in His Word that He daily adds to us.

> Blessed be the Lord, Who daily loads us with benefits, the God of our salvation! (Psalm 68:19)

Each and every day is a day in your season that can be lived in perfection and favor. We have heard it said, "God is more interested in the destination." That being true does not take away from the fact that He is just as much interested in the details of our journeys. Every day has meaning and purpose. It is to your benefit to live each day's agenda as God desires. He makes all things good in their time. Don't buy into the idea that since your good thing is coming, you simply wait for it to come. He has an ever-increasing abundance for your life. This is in regards to spiritual and physical blessings. There is specific timing for certain gifts from God, but He is not at all interested in your complacency for those gifts. He wants you to grow in the knowledge of Him, and all the while reaping His benefits.

If He has made you a promise, don't make it the focal point of your life. Don't let it tie you down from everything else God wants to bless you with. When you do obsess over gifts, you are serving not the God of Abraham, Isaac and Jacob, but the god of self. I personally believe God will withhold further or certain blessings if you don't properly steward the ones He already gave you. If He blesses you with a dream job and it takes over your life, what good has come of it? God wanted to satisfy you and give you your heart's desire, but you turned it for evil. Not only will this hinder God's work in your life, but you will be dissatisfied with what you already have. We will be set free when we realize God makes everything good in its time. We will enjoy what we currently have, knowing He makes each day new.

Today is the day of your favor; He has not only given you Jesus, but all things with Him. It is your choice to release His favor into your life. The error comes when we are not aware of the season we are in. We can miss many good things God has prepared for us. You must learn to discern your season, because every day brings different things. A.W. Tozer once said, "We'll hardly get our feet out of time into eternity that we'll bow our heads in shame and humiliation. We'll gaze on eternity and say, 'Look at all the riches there were in Jesus Christ, and I've come to the Judgment Seat almost a pauper" (Leonard Ravenhill). For God had not only given us Jesus Christ, but He has with Him freely given us all things (Romans 8:32).

I challenge Christians today to discern their season. Recognize what God is doing in your heart. Realize His work in the circumstances of your life. When you realize His work, you will begin to understand your life and God's current vision. It will give you perspective on what the next step is. You will see that the Lord has been leading you. It is your cooperation that is critical. As we examine peoples' lives today, how many can we honestly say are living with destination, purpose, and an eternal perspective? Instead of living with destiny, people tend to live complacent lives because they spend their seasons alone, making the decision not to accept the responsibility God has placed on them. You are and will continue to be a direct result of what you sow (Galatians 6:7). If you want to live with an eternal perspective, accept this challenge and you shall see "great and mysterious things" (Jeremiah 33:3).

Furthermore, there are seasons that we go through that were never meant for us to go through. There are situations we go through simply because we brought ourselves there. It is not God who condones such behavior; therefore He cannot be blamed for them. We were never meant to walk through certain valleys but we begin to go through dark places when we leave the boundaries of the Word of God. The Bible states, "Your word is a lamp to my feet and a light to my path" (Psalm 119:105). The Word of God is meant to safeguard us from danger, whether it is physical or emotional. Some people are led into great deception when they can't let go of their past. One major reason they can't let go is because they can't understand why it happened to them, so they accept it as fate, something unavoidable. However, if you start to realize why one gets hurt, it has nothing to do with God.

Imagine a sheepfold that is safeguarded by a hedge. The master built the hedge to protect the sheep from any danger, but if a young sheep finds its way around the gate and goes off into the wilderness, it is lost. As the sun sets, it gets colder. The sheep hasn't had anything to eat. It whimpers, cold and hungry. The emotional damage has already been done to the sheep, but the ordeal continues. The sheep falls into a ditch and wounds itself even more because it sees not where it goes. Coyotes and wolves begin to howl through the night. It is not only hurt, but now traumatized. The longer the sheep stays in the wilderness, the further wounded it becomes. Back at home, the master notices a sheep is missing. He grabs his cloak and hurries off into the dark, hoping the sheep hasn't been killed yet. He searches for hours, hopeful he will find the missing sheep. Suddenly he hears a whimper, and turning around he sees the sheep curled up in a ditch, shivering. The master sweeps the sheep into his arms, comforting the wounded and scared animal. The master nurtures and comforts the sheep as they journey home. Though the sheep knows it is safe, it will live with that experience for the rest of its life. The emotional wounds of fear are much greater than physical scars. The healing has to be significant.

It is the same in our lives when we leave the Master's protection. If we stay in the hedge of God's Word, we will find protection and comfort. We will avoid many situations that would only bring us hurt and confusion. However, anything that scarred our lives can be restored. God can remove all fear and pain from our lives if we allow Him to. We have no reason to hold onto our pains if we have the One who died to heal us. Close the doors of your past by allowing the Holy Spirit to release you from it through repentance, forgiveness, and renewal of the mind. Meditate on the Word of God; as you begin to establish the truths of God's Word in your heart you will be transformed in soul and body.

A Word in Every Season

Understanding the current season you are in also reveals the current word God has placed in your heart. Every child of God carries a particular *word* in any given season. A word can be a revelation, an affirmation, a promise, a scripture, etc. This word first grows in your heart, changing you, but then it is for the "edifying of the saints" (Ephesians 4:12).

To illustrate this, we all know certain individuals that at one point or another repeated the same revelation or word, over and over. I used to find this very irritating, but the Lord said to me, "I have given that individual a word that has to be released; how he or she releases it is through their own personality." In that instance, I understood one of the ways God fulfills His purposes on earth: He places a word in every individual for every season's purpose.

You have a word that needs to be released and shared with others today. You may be releasing it, not aware. You may be conducting yourself in a way that is speaking to someone, but you are completely oblivious. The take-away here is that every child of God has a plan and purpose that is connected to the body of Christ for edification. If we don't walk in our callings, we are missing out on blessing others as well as ourselves.

The Kingdom of God surely advances, but as mentioned earlier, your part in it depends on your cooperation. We are here for each other, and God uses us for one another's benefit. Be aware of your influence, because wherever you go, you are influencing others. Don't be concerned with how God will bring His will to pass, because He always does. He has even spoken through unbelievers to carry out His will. There are mentions in scripture where the Holy Spirit spoke through various unbelievers and even a donkey (Numbers 22:28; John 11:49-50). He is greater than we can ever imagine; His ways are perfect. Therefore, let us live as open vessels for the cause of Christ, releasing the word He has given us in every season. Do not concern yourself with the word you need to share, but simply love Jesus, and follow your heart. When you love Jesus with all your heart, your life will fall seamlessly into God's perfect will.

†

Chapter 7
Devotion

Imagine that in today's world, every individual lives off a battery pack that keeps him or her alive. Every few weeks the individual has to go to a battery source to recharge their battery; if they don't, they will die. Without getting too technical, the battery is one's life. Every person in this world feeds off something to give them *life*. Some choose to chase the pleasures of the world while others live quietly. They live complacently by enjoying life somewhere in the middle of extreme and passive. However, none of these extremes or balances will give an individual *life*. People can keep pursuing what they *think* gives them life, but the source of life is found only in God. No matter how great your achievements will be, they will never satisfy you. There is nothing that will give you peace or purpose but knowing God.

> *And this is eternal life, that they may know You, the only true God, and Jesus Christ whom you have sent.* (John 17:3)

We have all seen people gain riches and fame, all the while remaining unhappy and depressed. People will never be satisfied in anything this world can offer because people were made in the image of God. In a sense, people cannot exist separated completely from God. The source of life is in God, and it is His breath that gives man life. The only reason we exist is because at one point in time, God breathed life into Adam. The breath of life was passed down into every generation, giving life to every child that was born. We see the evidence of God everywhere through the existence of our family, friends, and peers. We would not and cannot exist apart from God.

> For in Him we live and move and have our being, as also some of your poets have said, 'For we are also His offspring.' (Acts 17:28)

Life exists in your spirit man, that born-again part of you. Without your spirit, you would cease to exist physically. So if we lead a life that strengthens our spirit man, are we not simultaneously giving life to our flesh?

> It will be health to your flesh, and strength to your bones.
> (Proverbs 3:8)

When you connect to God, you will gain vitality not only in your soul, but also in your physical body. There is a lot published today on the laws of happiness and attraction, and they all have one thing in common: you are what you *think* you are. They are right in this regard. If you believe what the Word says about you, you will be transformed into the likeness of Christ. As the Holy Spirit makes the scripture alive to you, it will bring *life* to you. Your soul will experience the life force behind all things.

> It is the Spirit who gives life; the flesh profits nothing. The words that I speak to you are spirit, and they are life. (John 6:63)

> To be carnally minded is death, but to be spiritually minded is life and peace. (Romans 8:6)

If you do your own research, you will begin to see that the vitality of your existence begins and ends in your spirit. When scripture refers to the Spirit, it is speaking about the Holy Spirit. However, a born-again believer's spirit is connected to the Spirit, and being joined gives the spirit life. It is of great benefit to understand this. It is wisdom that brings understanding on many matters of life.

To put it into perspective, let's look at the world around us. People are dying, corrupt and in need of saving. Their "batteries" are long overdue for a recharge. People need *life*, but *life* is found only in God. No amount of money, fame, or even charitable works will give them life. They need the true life force to be rejuvenated. If people explore the truth of life and seek that truth, God will reveal Himself to them. As they step towards God, they will drink from the well of living water, never thirsting again (John 4:14).

Searching for Silver

The word of God says that those that seek God as they would for silver will find Him. *And if you seek her as silver, and search for her as for hidden treasures; then you will understand the fear of the Lord, and find the knowledge of God* (Proverbs 2:4).

Imagine someone came up to you right now and told you that there was silver hidden in the very room you were in. Would you not drop everything and search for it until you found it? We all would. The Word of God says that in the same manner we must look for Him. God is challenging our values here. He knows money defines value in our world and He compares Himself to it. In our monetary system, silver and gold are precious commodities. God gets right down to the bottom of what's important to us and compares Himself to it, revealing the true desires of our hearts.

Now you may protest, "How could you compare God to money!" But I ask you, what do you work harder for, God or money? Everything being in its place, we don't pursue God in the same manner that we pursue money. Spending quality and quantity time with God is the way to find Him. Scripture is full of passages that speak on seeking God. All of them summed up say, "If you seek Me with a whole heart, you will find Me" (Deuteronomy 4:29). But many Christians complain about not hearing or seeing God and conclude that He is far away. However, His Word says that if you don't search for Him, you will not experience Him. It is not about the time spent, but the condition of your heart. Seeking means searching and searching *until* you find Him, and I assure you all that's required is a humble heart. Such a heart will seek until it finds the treasure. A passive heart will not get far with God. He desires a devoted, hungry and reverent heart. You cannot pursue God indifferent and unresponsive. He loves you and desires to come to you, but He is limited to your faith in Him.

For he who comes to God must believe that He is. (Hebrews 11:6)

†

Chapter 8
A Lifestyle

It is difficult to find great examples nowadays. Even among Christians, there is a lack of examples to look up to. Many of our own friends fell away from the faith. Some made a scene while others gradually fell away. As I grew older, this dilemma troubled me. My desire was to understand exactly why Christians fell away from the faith. Then suddenly I began to realize that faith is a decision. I began to see that no amount of miracles or signs would persuade a person to believe in God. Yes, they inspire us and are great experiences, but they do not seal one's faith in God. What seals one's faith is a decision.

Let's take a look at John the Baptist who, at his final hours, questioned whether Jesus was indeed the Christ. Out of all people, why would John the Baptist question the One he prepared the road for? Did John not see all the miracles Jesus performed? But at that final hour of his life, those miracles and signs were far gone from his mind and heart. Jesus reassured Him by pointing to the signs and miracles that were occurring, but it was not the signs that caused John to believe, it was the Christ. John kept his faith upon Jesus to the end. The key point to realize is that the signs and miracles still left doubt in John's mind. Faith is not found in physical sight.

What causes you to believe in God? Is it the miracles that convince you? If you assume you would believe in God if He gave you signs, then you have something else coming. You can have one experience after another, which can bless you, but in time those miracles will diminish. If your faith is staked on miracles, it will lose its ground.

Faith is not found in the miracles, but in a decision to trust God. The definition of faith is the evidence of things unseen (Hebrews 11:1). In simplest terms, faith is the confident belief in what we cannot see. If faith is a confident belief in what we *cannot* see, then how could the things that we *do* see give us faith? It is not found in physical sight; it is found in the heart. It is with the heart that man can truly see, for the heart is faith's eyes.

For with the heart one believes unto righteousness. (Romans 10:9)

To believe with your heart means to make a decision in your heart. Your heart is irrelevant to your physical sense of sight. Therefore, we must base our trust in God solely by faith. We cannot choose to trust Him when we see signs and wonders, because even if we do, it will not profit us. It is with the heart that one believes, not by physical sight. Once we make that decision, our faith becomes a seed that God waters. When we make that step towards God, He will cause our faith to grow. However if there is no seed, nothing can grow. As scripture shows us, there is nothing that can bring us toward God more so than making a free will decision to believe.

Without faith, it is impossible to please God. (Hebrews 11:6)

On the other hand, if you keep coming back to what is visible, you will find it very hard to believe in God because He is of the spirit. Those that come to him must come in spirit and truth (John 4:24). We must come to a place where we say, "No matter what I see or hear, I choose to believe in God. I don't believe in myself. I don't believe in my ability to understand truth, but I believe in God to show me." That kind of faith God will reward.

Abraham and Isaac

In the Bible we read the story of God instructing Abraham to kill Isaac as a sacrifice. The Lord showed me a vision regarding that story. I found myself observing Abraham and Isaac hiking up the mountain, and Abraham carrying a dagger on his side. I continued to watch and noticed that Abraham was in great distress. Isaac was running alongside him, excited to be on the trip. Isaac began asking his dad if they could go on another trip the week after, like any young boy would. All Abraham could do was smile and say, "Yes son." I then realized what God was showing me. Abraham did not leave the question about what to do with Isaac undecided. He chose to trust God even before they began the hike.

Now, imagine if Abraham had not resolved to obey God. What would happen if Isaac began telling his dad about all the journeys they would be taking in the future and the good times they would experience? This would break any father's heart, and if he had not made his decision to obey God ahead of time, this might have broken him down. Although he struggled with the decision he had made, his decision sustained his heart and the Lord rewarded Abraham for it. God had no intention of killing Isaac, but only to mature Abraham's faith. We later read that Abraham's faith was counted to him as righteousness (Romans 4:5). Abraham was saved because of his faith. God needed to bring real faith out of Abraham to cause him to be saved. What an extraordinary God!

That's why it is important to live by faith and not by sight (2 Corinthians 5:7). If sight gave us faith, God would reveal more than enough angels to us. Even if heaven were revealed to your physical eyes, it wouldn't add faith to you. Jesse Duplantis had such an encounter, which he testified about some time ago. When asked if seeing heaven gave him more faith, Jesse replied that it did not. Yet how often do we say, "Lord just show me something!" or "If I could only see heaven, I would believe!" This is erroneous faith. I have heard many testimonies of heavenly experiences and supernatural encounters, yet not one person said it increased their faith. Otherwise, faith wouldn't be faith. Faith is taking a risk for God, not knowing in the *natural man* what it is.

We also know of unbelievers that experienced God in some way, who saw miracles happen before their very eyes, yet they weren't convinced of God's existence. They write it off as something they can't explain, because they never will understand it through their natural senses. If they cannot comprehend it physically, they don't know what else to do with it. Faith opens the valve of your spirit man, which in turn brings understanding.

In order to truly change, one must accept Jesus by faith, which is a simple decision of the heart. Faith is found in your free choice. When we make that step, God is greatly pleased because we chose Him over our own understanding (Proverbs 3:5) and nothing pleases Him more (Hebrews 11:6). Even after you are born-again by faith, you will need to keep walking in faith of what God speaks to you. Only after you step out in faith will you prove the work of God. With time, our faith in God becomes stronger and we don't hesitate to believe what God speaks to us, but it will *always* require your action.

Dear children, make that decision of faith. Your decision gives the Holy Spirit access to your life. The Spirit will place your decision on a rock, where it cannot be moved. So yes, it is our choice to make, but it is God who keeps us to the end. A willing heart is all that he needs. Glory to God!

There is one such man who experienced this first-hand. Rees Howells was a called intercessor of his time. In his book, he goes into detail about a very difficult time of his life, when the Holy Spirit brought him to a stalemate. Rees was a man of great spiritual stature who worked with the Lord for the salvation of many souls. God began to speak to him about surrendering his life further. Rees thought about all the sacrifices he had already made; he didn't understand how he could surrender any more. He trembled at the thought of what the Holy Spirit was asking him to do, and he struggled for weeks with this decision. Finally the Holy Spirit motioned to him, "By this time tomorrow, you must make your decision. You will have no more time." From that moment, each hour seemed to drag longer than the previous, each hour tormenting him. He was unsure how to surrender any further, and He wondered whether the Lord was asking him to die.

The next day, the Spirit spoke to him again, saying, "Your time is approaching." (This is a very exceptional story that you must re-read yourself in his book to understand his life and what the Spirit was doing). Reese continued to struggle, paralyzed with fear and worry. He heard the Spirit say, "One minute." By this point, Rees began to panic.

Then at the last second he cried out, "Lord I cannot! I am willing! I am willing! If only I could, I would! But I am unable!" The Holy Spirit whispered back, "That's all I need, a willing heart."

What a work God does! He knows we are unable to surrender on our own, so instead all that he asks for is our willingness to surrender. We cannot change on our own, but when we choose to surrender, He will change us. He will affirm our decision and keep us. We have no power to keep ourselves faithful, but He does. He listens to the murmurs of our hearts and responds to them. What a wonderful God we serve!

In the book, "Secrets of the Silence," Bob Kilpatrick writes, "There is a secret; when we come before Him in silence, God answers even the prayers we never pray. God listens to our hearts. Even more encouraging, He already knows our needs and is more than willing to guide and provide for us." Though we have needs and desires, we need to trust the Holy Spirit to take care of us. When we have questions that need answers, the Holy Spirit will answer them. When He does, it will be like a double-edged sword (Hebrews 4:12), exposing every aspect of the dilemma and leaving no room for further questions.

A Lifestyle of Faith

We have heard it said that to be spiritually minded is life and peace, but to be carnally minded is death (Romans 8:6). Christians worldwide live carnal lifestyles. They live in the usual routine of Sunday services, but they don't live an actual lifestyle of faith. The first thing to note is that faith is aggressive (Matthew 11:12); it requires your total commitment and dependence on God. Faith calls you to action. It is not complacent. It is not fearful of man. More than anything else, faith values God's opinion above all. Christians will not have successful, "Christ-like" lives until they make faith a lifestyle.

For many, church rather than faith is a lifestyle. They have it all wrong. We supposedly seek God, but I question the actuality of this. Faith believes in an invisible God. It is patient and confident in which it believes. Living a lifestyle of faith comes from a decision. That decision is not dependent on the emotions you experience today or tomorrow;

rather it is a faith versus miracle mentality. The miracle mentality seeks a sign from God to believe, but faith is a lifestyle, not a lifeline. People seek God when a tragedy occurs, but God is teaching us that it's the lifestyle that needs to be changed. God is merciful and takes care of those that humbly cry out to him, but I submit to you that He wants a people that continually walk by faith. He does not want a people that desert Him when all is well, who only come running back when their enemies return. He desires a nation that acknowledges Him as God, day and night. In "Worthy of it All," David Brymer sings, "Day and night, night and day, let incense arise." Let the incense of our worship and praise go to Him all the days of our lives. God knows that if we learn a lifestyle of faith, we will always walk in peace and confidence. He desires for us to walk in power! This isn't God demanding honor; this is God demanding your peace!

Instead of a faith lifestyle, fear is more common nowadays. We let fear drive us to God but God isn't found in fear or worry. On the contrary, fear hinders God. In his book "The Soul-Winning Century," Rex Humbard wrote: "Worrying is not faith. You cannot worry and have faith at the same time, as one of them has to cease in order for the other to work." Jesus commanded us not to worry, but this is only possible through a faith lifestyle. Faith does not worry! Faith lives in the peace and joy of the presence of God.

Our faith should be a *response*, not a reaction. A *response* is a way of life, a protocol. It already knows what it will do in every situation. A response is established in the heart; such a heart is always at peace. Jesus was sleeping during the storm at sea, and even when His disciples finally woke Him up, He remained at peace. He rebuked the storm as well as their lack of faith. His peace was not compromised by it. We too are meant to have the same response Jesus did. We can experience peace during our storms, but if we simply react to what happens, we will be unstable and unsure in our ways. A reaction is afraid and worrisome. We must transition ourselves to a faith lifestyle.

Today, establish your decision on the Word of God, and let it rule your heart and mind. The Word of God will make faith a permanent presence in your heart, but the people of God have to also re-establish it in their homes. We were purchased for a price and made new, but now to live this new life, we must surrender our old ways of life. We can no longer continue in the pattern of the world. How can one walk by faith without the Word of God? It is impossible, because the Word of God is the roadmap for faith. We say we want to live for God, but walking with God requires knowing His Word. We cannot walk by faith if we have no road to guide us. When living by sight, we have physical walls to guide us. We live by what we see. If you choose to walk by faith, you cannot just tear down physical walls without first establishing spiritual walls. Physical walls are the customs of this world. Spiritual walls are the principles of the Kingdom.

If you choose God, you must abide in His Word. If you choose the world, you already know the customs of the world and will have no problem living by them. Christians cannot live in both worlds. One's desire to live for the world won't be hindered by God, but one's desire to live for God will be hindered by the world. To live a supernatural lifestyle requires an establishment of the truth of the Word of God.

The primary truth of the Word of God is that Jesus Christ is Lord. Furthermore, He is the Word of God; the Bible simply represents Him. To live a Christian life, one must know the King of the Christian faith. Without the king, you cannot have the kingdom. You cannot maintain a life of prayer and the Word if your focus isn't completely on Jesus. You will either walk in a carnal mind or a spiritual mind. A spiritual mind is a reflection of the Word of God. To walk spiritually is more than just going through the motions. It's about taking an aggressive faith approach. It's not just about knowing scripture, because the Word of God is spiritual matter. When mixed with faith, the words have power. They are experiential revelations. They are truths and principles of the Kingdom of God. They reveal the spirit man. Many of these truths become revelations to us when we wait upon God and allow Him to reveal them to us. Revelation is not in your hands. It is the Spirit's prerogative to shed light upon your mind. You have no power to do so otherwise. Seek God and He will reveal Himself to you (1 Chronicles 28:9).

Allow the Spirit to speak to you the message of this chapter today. It is the core issue of our Christian faith. Without faith, we have nothing. Therefore, submit yourselves to God and resist the devil (James 4:7). Jesus had a lifestyle of faith, hope and love. He was the full potential of what a Christian can be. He didn't just represent virtues; He was the very essence of them. We are co-heirs with Him and are to be like Him. You can move forward in the likeness of Christ to attain faith, hope, and love. These virtues are spirit and they are life (John 6:63). One cannot have the fullness of faith, hope and love without Christ. To have Christ is to have all, for Christ is all (Colossians 3:11).

A Lifestyle of Love

I want to show you an illustration of the love of Christ. When He was put on trial, imagine the people that mocked and spat at Him, jeering and shouting their hateful comments. Now imagine this: these hateful words, as they were being released from the mouths of people, instantly burned at the touch of His face. His love towards them was so pure that it consumed evil. As it says in the Word, "Love will cover a multitude of sins" (1 Peter 4:8). Jesus did not even consider the facet of offense. Love does not need to refrain from getting angry because it loves without offense. Christ had a lifestyle of love, and love reigned within His heart. His response was love. True love is unconditional and endures all things. Jesus was trained in the ways of God because He knew God and He was God. He was unmoved by evil.

God calls us to be the same as Jesus. We can trust that love will always have more power than any facet of evil because in the spiritual realm, love has legal authority over evil. I have heard stories of Christians that would hug a demon-possessed individual to cast the demon out; it drives them away (1 John 4:18). Love is unmatched by any force.

But above all, put on love. (Colossians 3:14)

A Lifestyle of Praise and Thanksgiving

Along with faith and love, a heart of gratitude has to become a lifestyle. A grateful heart is one that praises God before a gift is received. Praise and thanksgiving come from the heart, just like faith. True reverence is thanking the Lord ahead of a blessing. It is much better to honor God before you receive a gift than afterwards because peace and joy don't come from the gift—they come by faith. It is not enough to praise God after the fact. As Jesus said, even evil fathers give their children good gifts. In the same way, even evil people praise God when they are blessed. But God is after a people that will praise Him in every moment of their lives, regardless of what state they are in. He honors those that honor Him.

Learn to give sacrificial praise over *reaction* praise. Honor God in those times when you don't have what you need, because this brings great joy to the Father. When there is a sacrifice, there is faith. While "not having," praise God, so when you receive what you need, sacrificial praise will create a grateful heart in you. Out of a grateful heart, praise and thanksgiving flow. He is our Father and will take care of every need, but there is no faith in honoring Him only when all is good.

Throughout your life, you will give and receive from God. If you only give praise after you receive, that praise has no weight. Such praises are short-lived and come from an ungrateful heart. God honors those praises that resonate within our hearts. We must learn to be living sacrifices by continually offering praise and thanksgiving regardless of our circumstances (Romans 12:1). Our reverence to God will only be as abundant as it is in our hearts.

Chapter 9
The Will of God is Your Greatest Happiness

There is no greater joy than being in the Will of God. Living in His will brings complete peace, and you will bask in the benefits of it. Many Christians fear the Will of God, assuming it will make them do things they don't want to. They are gravely mistaken. That mentality says everything about your philosophy of God. If you actually believed God is good, you would not hesitate a moment to accept His will for your life. The problem with many of us believers is that we have not believed what the Word of God says about God. Rather, we continue to view God through our own philosophies.

My personal experience with the Will of God has changed my life completely. In my life I had always sought God, but not wholeheartedly. You will only find so much of God with that attitude. I would say, "God, fulfill this desire and I will do anything for you." This would re-occur in my life. Whatever I wanted at the time, I thought I should have it before I served God. I thought I was very persuasive, and I would say, "God you know that if I get this, I will completely serve you, with nothing holding me back." I actually thought I was doing God a favor, but little did I realize God was patiently working in my heart.

One night in a prayer meeting, I sensed the Spirit's presence as if a light had illuminated my mind. The very philosophy I had been practicing in my life was being exposed. The Holy Spirit showed me how my understanding of God did not line up with His Word. I realized the erroneous philosophy I had about God. I had also made God an enemy by positioning my heart against Him and demanding my terms. All things are brought to exposure in His presence. I had not realized how naïve I had been, and it became evident to me that I was telling God I would not serve Him unless He gave me what I wanted. However, God does not take half-hearted people alongside Him.

This breakthrough also exposed my philosophy on God's nature. By thinking I needed something to actually serve Him, I was saying that God is not perfect and that God's will doesn't suffice for all my needs and desires. How wrong I was! The Holy Spirit instantly showed me that the Will of God for my life is beyond good and it will only bless me. When I grasped this truth, I let go of all my desires and replaced them for God's will. It was definitely hard coming to that point, but by the power of the Holy Spirit, it was completely possible. I realized the difficulty laid in the fact that I did not trust God. We don't trust God when He says He has a great life planned for us. We don't trust Him when He says, "Seek first the Kingdom and all else will be added to you" (Matthew 6:33). If we simply took Him at His word, we would have no problem surrendering our lives to Him, knowing full well that he would take care of us.

My fellow brothers and sisters in Christ, *that* is the secret of why it is so difficult to let go. It is impossible for a rich man to enter heaven because the rich man does not trust God. Instead, he puts his trust in money (Matthew 19:23) and does not do the Will of God. Foremost, the Will of God for our lives is to be a living sacrifice, which means surrendering all to Him. Jesus said, "If you love Me, you will obey my commandments" (John 14:15). He also said to the rich young man, "With God all things are possible" (Matthew 19:26); it is possible for anyone to enter the Kingdom.

At first, I thought it was impossible to let go of the desires I had for a better life, but the Holy Spirit made it clear to me that God was for me and not against me; all I had to do was believe that He had my best interests at heart. Once I believed this, I was able to let go and trust Him as My provider. It is at these pinnacle moments of our lives that God begins to work. Everything begins to work for our good when we surrender to Him (Matthew 6:33).

Chapter 10
If it is of Faith, It will Succeed

And now I say to you, keep away from these men and let them alone; for if this plan or this work is of men, it will come to nothing; but if it is of God, you cannot overthrow it—lest you even be found to fight against God.
(Acts 5:38-39)

I want every Christian to understand a basic truth: *If it is of faith, it will succeed. If it is of man, it will fail.* This should give you not only hope but also encouragement in your walk with God. If what you plan to do is not of God, it will run its course and die. I am speaking in regards to any endeavor in life. When we are saved by grace through faith, we step into God's provision. We step off the path of destruction and step on the path of mercy, favor and provision. The following verse clearly points to the fact that those who love God and actively seek His will are on God's path of favor and provision.

> *And we know that all things work together for good to those who love God, to those who are the called according to His purpose.*
> (Romans 8:28)

However, what tends to happen is that we continue to live our lives as if we were never saved. We may not necessarily live sinful lives, but we don't renew our minds to the Word of God. What will happen to a person like that? Think about it: they "chose" the Will of God, by becoming born-again, but they continue to live by their own will. It's a contradictory lifestyle. You cannot tear down physical walls unless you replace them with spiritual walls. My point is that a Christian's actions and words are now contingent upon their faith. To live by faith requires us to know what the Word of God says! We have to accept who we are in Christ to live successful Christian lives. It is completely opposite with unbelievers. They are not in the Will of God, so the things they do don't necessarily coincide with faith. Though something may work for them, it is irrelevant to their faith because they are not on God's path.

On the other hand, a Christian is on God's path. What they do with their lives matters a lot more because they are bestowed with an inheritance in Jesus Christ and "seated in heavenly places with Christ" (Ephesians 2:6). One cannot serve both Satan and God. For what do light and darkness have in common (2 Corinthians 6:14)? They go head-to-head in battle, yet very few Christians realize the significance and importance of their born-again lives. If you operate in faith, you will see God's hand provide for you. However when you are enticed of your own lust to do something (James 1:14), it will rarely give you any joy or success.

Lust is obsession and doubt. Lust doubts the grace of God by ignoring that God will provide everything in good time. When you operate out of lust, you don't trust God's goodness. You feel like you need something that God can't provide for you, so you chase after it. The desires of your heart are meant to be fulfilled, but what those desires are can be misunderstood if you are not making God your priority.

The closer we are to God, the more of ourselves we become, so it is vital to make God our ultimate pursuit. God wants to be involved in every part of our lives. He blesses our endeavors and choices, but He always knows the best choice to make. As we draw near to God, we will know those choices by instinct. Our experiences will be the direct result of our choices. If we allow God to lead us in our choices, we will experience God's best.

However, many things we attempt in life are not in the Will of God, therefore very often we find ourselves discouraged in failures. I am speaking about any endeavor in life. Again, I point you to the fact that God is perfect, and He desires for you to be like Him (Matthew 5:48).

Another point to note is that we consist of God. God lives in and through us (Acts 17:28). We exist because His breath gives us life. So when we choose His plans, we are choosing the best pathway for our lives (Psalm 32:8). It is not a matter of doing what God wants us to do, but a matter of doing what we were originally designed for. God desires his influence in every part of society. You can be an actor or actress in Hollywood, but instead religion teaches us to stay in church and lock the doors. Doing things out of faith is not at all limited to church matters. For example, God can lead a businessman to make the best decisions for his business, including day-to-day operations, long term investments, and so on. This will require the businessman's faith in what he believes God is speaking to him. As he walks by faith, his capacity to hear and do as God says will grow. I am illustrating the point of living with the Holy Spirit as your advisor on all matters. The Word of God represents the perfection of God and the glorious life Christians should be experiencing in this day and age, as a foretaste of what's to come.

A good friend of mine was thinking about moving out-of-state to Florida. If he had chosen to move-away, I would miss him, but I desire the Will of God for every man and woman. I blessed him in my heart, but when I heard him talk about Florida and moving out-of-state, I immediately heard the Holy Spirit say to me, *if it is of man, it will fail. If it is of faith, it will succeed.* God was not saying that this was a mistake, but He was telling me that we should make all our decisions based on faith. We should never make choices out of spite. We should pursue excellence in all that we do. Pursuing excellence is pursuing God's will. I don't mean to say that you have to be perfect for God, but that you should pursue to be like God. He is not lazy or passive. Our God is determined and excellent, so in all that you do, imitate God. He knows what you need and when you need it. He knows the plans He has for you and the best pathway to it (Psalm 32:8). This isn't about God having His way, but about you having *your* way. The idea of a demanding God is a great misconception. He's not in it for Himself; He's in it for us. Why else would Jesus lay down His life, if not for our sake (John 10:10)? It is to God's glory for us to live in faith, because

He will prove Himself to the world through us. As we continually operate in faith, it is not only to our advantage, but also to the glory of God. In all matters, we are to glorify Him, because it is all about Him (Colossians 3:11). It is God whom we serve and live for. Living by faith is not simply to get what we want, but to glorify God as we witness His glory in our lives.

We may not always live by faith, but we need to remain hopeful even when we make a wrong move because *all things work together for good to those who love God and are called according to His purpose* (Romans 8:28). God will re-direct our steps onto the right path when we are sidetracked, but we should learn to obey and follow His orders promptly, so that we don't walk through valleys we don't have to. This will bring the most success to your life. I am not preaching "success" but the success of God in your life. God never fails, but you do. You fail when you don't walk by faith; you fail when you choose your way over God's. Remember, God has the best plan for your life, but don't idolize that statement. Christianity is not necessarily an easy path in life. We will face trials and tribulations because we live in a fallen world. However we will not have to trudge through it as the world does, because we have the *mind of Christ* (1 Corinthians 2:16) and the power of the Holy Spirit (Acts 1:8).

God desires a good and worry-free life for us (Matthew 6:25), but for some reason Christians continue to believe that we have to suffer in life to please God. Nothing could be further from the truth. We should not be exalting materialism by giving it that power. For example, to some people poverty is an idol. They rebuke the wealthy, standing behind their lack and professing that it brings glory to God. This is self-righteousness and dead religion. God is far from such hypocrites. It is neither poverty nor wealth that glorifies God, but a *living sacrifice.* Our priority is not our needs, but the Kingdom.

> *Seek first the Kingdom and all these things shall be added unto you.* (Matthew 6:33)

Only those that love God and live according to His purpose will experience a successful life (Psalms 1:3). There are many who love to make arguments against fellow Christians who believe God does desire to bless His people but it is only because they are proud and selfish. They attribute success to self-gain, but to a genuine Christian, personal success means Kingdom success.

One area of life many stumble in is money. Many don't believe God wants you to be rich for one very ignorant reason: they think it is selfish. But what if you're not selfish? Is money still a blessing or a curse? Many would continue to say that money is the root of evil. I have one question for them: are you rooted in Christ or in the world? If you are rooted in Christ, money is no evil to you. If you are rooted in the world, money is the least of your problems. Everything will be a curse to you, because without God you have no *life*. The fundamental question presented here is the true allegiance of your heart. More money in my life means more money for the Kingdom. To a carnal person, more money means more luxuries. God does not mind luxuries, but He minds where your heart is. If He has your heart, He has everything.

If you operate out of faith daily, you will experience personal success. It will benefit you because what you attempt to do will be of God. On the contrary, when you chase after your own lust, it will run into the ground. Sin brings death. Chasing your own pleasure or ideas may not necessarily be bad, but bring little or no result. I am not saying we shouldn't pursue an idea or project, but I am offering an alternative, pursuing the *right* ideas and projects. What good is it to invest time and effort into something that is not sure to succeed? This applies to all decisions in life. Never make a decision without basing it on your faith. If you continually operate in faith, God will lead you to the right decision. Why pursue a carnal will? Don't you realize that you have died to yourself and been made alive to Christ? We have all experienced failures in our lives, but re-examine yours: *how many of those endeavors have been God-led?* By hearing many Christians talk about their experiences, I see that much that goes on is done out of mere human intention rather than divine wisdom. This is why we experience very little success as Christians. We have not given ourselves over to God. My friends, whatever your experience or philosophy is, you must remember that God never fails. If God told you to do something, whether it worked out or not, it's not God's failure. If anything, you failed. You failed at completely trusting Him in it. You failed at continuing to walk and adhere to His voice. From this day forward, be encouraged that when "it is out of faith, no one can fight against it" (Acts 5:38), because God is unstoppable.

Learn to discern His voice and the word He speaks to you. It is also a continual process of refinement that will help you discern His voice. Your *faith capacity* will expand as your relationship with Him grows.

In my personal relationship with Jesus, He would say time and time again, *if it is of faith it will succeed, if it is of man it will fail.* He wanted me to understand why our plans fail. I am not sure what God's intention was for my friend who wanted to move out-of-state, but I know that this is a revelation the Holy Spirit wanted to share with His beloved church regarding our endeavors in life. If we love God, we will obey Him (John 14:15). You will desire His will and not your own.

A mature Christian can say that his or her desire to move geographically for example is already God's desire, because God changes our desires to His as we fellowship with Him. That's a true statement that I almost go without saying, because a mature Christian will already understand that. But I appeal more so to standard Christians, who don't seek the Will of God as much as they do their own way. You may be experiencing success or not but what I see in all this is the peace and confidence one can walk in if they live according to God's will. If you follow God, you will be content and at peace. It is not merely about having success, but about living in peace, joy and confidence. As one Russell Walden said to me, "Through simple obedience, He wants to deliver us from anxiety." Rest assured that you will experience success when you walk by faith. Believe and act upon His word today.

> So shall My word be that goes forth from My mouth; It shall not return to Me void, but it shall accomplish what I please, and it shall prosper in the thing for which I sent it. (Isaiah 55:11)

Chapter 11
True Desires

And the desire of the righteous will be granted. When the whirlwind passes by, the wicked is no more. But the righteous has an everlasting foundation. (Proverbs 10: 24)

When you love God with all your heart, you can assuredly follow the desires of your heart. The *desire of the righteous* refers to the desires of the spirit man. It is the *spirit* of a man that is righteous. No man in flesh is righteous, but because of Jesus Christ, we were made righteous through our spirits. Your spirit man is the only *righteous* part of you. Righteousness means "right standing with God." Those who have accepted Jesus as the ransom for their sins have been made right with Him. Not only do we have Jesus, but we have all things in Him, and as scripture states, *We have the mind of Christ* (1 Corinthians 2:16). Our spirit man is the man that Jesus is; we are just like Him before our Father. He looks upon us as He looks upon Jesus. *If you love Me, My Father loves you* (John 14:23). We can follow the desires of our spirits, because our spirit man is tied to Jesus Christ. As this verse states, the desires of the "righteous" will be granted, referring to our spirits.

The natural desires, visions, and talents we possess are in fact from your spirit man. That's why I say, *the closer you come to God, the more of yourself you become.* Your true desires are found in your spirit man. Surrender your life to God and live one day at a time, in peace and attentiveness, to what He will speak to you. *The natural will always gives birth*, meaning you will discover what you must do and want to do. It will surface as you tune into your spirit.

Naturally the things that keep resurfacing in our lives are the *desires* of our spirit, whatever they may be. For example, if you are designed to be an engineer, this will keep resurfacing in your life even if you become a doctor. The visions we see in our hearts are waiting to be born. God knows your potential, and He has placed visions and dreams within you that are waiting in eager expectation to be discovered. This is why I tend to say to people "you cannot separate yourself from God". Your *spirit*, born-again or not, was given to you by God. A *spirit* never ceases to exist. Once God speaks *life* into existence, it is forever. You can now begin to imagine how we are all connected to God, whether we like it or not. I can only imagine what God thinks when He sees His own *breath* denying Him.

> *Surely you have things turned around! Shall the potter be esteemed as the clay; for shall the thing made say of him who made it, "He did not make me"? Or shall the thing formed say of him who formed it, "He has no understanding"?* (Isaiah 29:16)

It is unreasonable to ask God why He made us; it is illogical to deny the existence of the one who created you. When we get past this illogic, we begin to understand how close we are to God. Even our natural desires are from Him. They are placed there by God. In the next chapter, written exclusively by my brother Michael, you will read more about pursuing your true desires.

Let's further examine the proverb. The next line says, *when the whirlwind passes by, the wicked is no more.* This is an analogy to the opposition we face in the world, though it is not always opposition but simply the disorder of the world. Sometimes, it's the unexpected stress we have to deal with or the unbelief that always challenges our faith. They are not of God, but of the devil. Satan brings chaos and disorder, but God brings peace and order. The implication here is that when everything passes by, the truth will remain. If you discover the blessings God has in store for you, but the affairs of the world temporarily blur your vision, don't be discouraged because you have an everlasting foundation. The Spirit knows who you are and He does not lie to you. If we seek after Him, and in turn follow the natural desires of our heart, we will unveil them.

Recall when God promised Abraham a son. No matter how impossible it seemed, even with time continually working against him, God still brought it into fulfillment. The truth of God's word to you will always be fulfilled. If you pursue God's vision for your life, you will have many projects, and as long as you walk with God, obeying Him every step, they will surely come to pass. Sometimes, we get a vision and instead of being patient on God, we go ahead of Him and try to fulfill it however we think is best. But God knows best. He knows what will or won't work. If you need financing, He knows the choice lenders and so on. God is not only interested in spiritual matters, but in every detail of our lives. To keep God in the church and out of our personal lives is to deny God entirely.

The final line of the passage goes on to say, *but the righteous has an everlasting foundation*. This means that no matter what's going on, God is above it. His plans will not go amiss. If He has placed a desire within you, that desire has the potential to be fulfilled. "You have an everlasting foundation" (Proverbs 10:24). Your desire comes from a solid place. It comes from a place that does not shake during a whirlwind. Though the whirlwind may temporarily blur things, it will pass and your desires will remain.

Paul wrote to the Corinthians, *the spiritual man discerns all things* (1 Corinthians 2:15). This further affirms my point that our spirits have the *mind of Christ* and are capable of anything. Bear in mind, this is because we are connected to the Holy Spirit. It is not us alone who can do anything, but as we operate from a spiritual mind, we can ascertain the best choices to make in our decisions.

What is of utmost importance in all this is our belief on what God speaks to us. If we don't make a decision to believe what He speaks to us, little more will be revealed. There is no point in God speaking more to you if you don't already believe what He has spoken. In the Garden of Eden, Satan understood the power was in the *Word*. God had spoken a word to Adam and Eve. God told them to eat of any fruit, except of the

Tree of the Knowledge of Good and Evil or they would surely die. Satan twisted God's words and began to say to Eve, *Has God said you would die? Has God said?* (Genesis 3:1). Lucifer knew that all he had to do was bring Eve to question God's *Word*. Everyone knows what happened next. Eve and Adam were both deceived, because they compromised what they had once believed. They began to doubt God's *Word*.

I can almost imagine how many Christians get frustrated when they hear that story. They vent, "Why, Adam and Eve? Why? How could you disobey the *word* God had clearly spoken to you? We would all be better off if you hadn't disobeyed!" Little do we realize, we repeat their mistake every day. Our consequences aren't as severe, but nevertheless they bring *death* to our spiritual lives. In varying degrees, we continue to doubt God's Word. There are secrets God desires to speak to us, but because we don't take the slightest step of faith to believe what He has already spoken, He will not speak more. *The secret of the Lord is with those who fear Him* (Psalm 25:14). God's heart only opens up to those who open up their hearts to Him. I am not talking about mercy and love, because God's mercy and love is open to all, but I am speaking about His counsels and mysteries. You will receive a breakthrough when you start to believe the little you have received from God, because He will exponentially give you more. But if you continue to refuse to believe, your heart will become dull of hearing, and the little you think you have will be taken away from you.

> And the disciples came and said to Him, "Why do You speak to them in parables?" He answered and said to them, "Because it has been given to you to know the mysteries of the kingdom of heaven, but to them it has not been given. For whoever has, to him more will be given and he will have abundance; but whoever does not have, even what he has will be taken away from him.

> Therefore I will speak to them in parables, because seeing they do not see, and hearing they do not hear, nor do they understand. And in them the prophecy of Isaiah is fulfilled, which says: 'Hearing you will hear and shall not understand, and seeing you will see and not perceive; for the hearts of the people have grown dull... Lest they should see with their eyes, lest they

should understand with their hearts and turn, so that I should heal them.'" (Matthew 13:10-15)

Jesus was speaking about people that don't accept His *words*. These are people that have the potential to *understand* and *perceive* but they choose not to, just as the Pharisees chose not to believe in the Christ because of their self-righteous spirit. Now the Lord is making another point here as well. He mentions, "Lest they should turn and be healed" (Matthew 13:15). I always asked myself, *why wouldn't God want them to repent?* But this is talking about something else entirely. The meaning behind that passage is that God will not manifest Himself to those that refuse to know Him. When you continually deny Christ, your heart grows duller to the truths of God's Word. There is great danger in making the *things of God* mundane. It's like taking a diamond and rubbing it in mud; it would lose its value to the naked eye. However, its value hasn't changed one bit. It is like this with God; the more we ignore His words, the less valuable they will seem to us. Can you imagine that the very words that carry *life* will lose their power? This will happen automatically if you act self-righteously as the Pharisees did. This will also happen if you don't act in faith of what God has spoken to you.

To guide our lives, there is first God's written Word, which contains principles and truths of the Kingdom of God. The fundamental truth in it is that Jesus Christ is Lord. Along with Christ, there are many more principles that follow. For example, one such principle is being a *generous giver* (2 Corinthians 8). That is a *word* God has already spoken to us. If we refuse to be generous givers, we are in fact refusing to obey His Word. God told Kent Mattox, "If you give Me your money, I know I've got your heart."

God also guides us by His verbal word, which is spoken to our hearts or spirits. One such example could be God putting it on my heart to join the usher ministry at my local church. If I keep ignoring this directive, I may lose the opportunity to step into the ministry, which is already a path for greater things, planned out by God. More than fulfilling a work, you will also continue to doubt God's word to you if you don't start to act in faith of what He has already spoken. If you do begin to move in it, your faith will grow and have the capacity to hear and see more from God. Your measure of faith is parallel to your measure of experience and responsibility.

Somewhere down the road, you will have to make a decision. You will have to decide whether you truly believe in God or not. If you choose to believe in God, that decision require risk by taking steps towards what God has spoken. Remember, there is no point in God speaking more to you if you don't already believe what He has spoken. But as you do walk by faith, you can trust your desires will be satisfied because they are born of the spirit. What the spirit desires is what God desires. Our spirit man has an *everlasting foundation* in Jesus Christ. We are the children of God and co-heirs with Christ. Walk as responsible stewards of this Gospel.

Chapter 12
Pursuing your Passion

By Michael Vilkhovoy

It is interesting to see that we were all made in the image of God, but yet we are all different. We all have different desires, interests, and hobbies, however we were all made for one purpose and that is to worship the living God and give him all the glory. In Colossians 3:17 it says, "Whatever you do in word or deed, do all in the name of the Lord Jesus, giving thanks through Him to God the Father." The problem is we feel that if we are not involved in church ministry, we cannot glorify God. There is an underlying issue when we feel the marketplace is not a place for God and that God cannot be glorified through our secular jobs. There is a mindset that we are missing God's perfect will if we aren't running a church or aren't in the mission field.

The church has done a terrible job in releasing people into their destinies and callings in life. We were all born with different desires and passions, those that are from God, and God wants us to pursue them with everything we have. If we are truly created in God's image, then those things inside of us that are beautiful to us, that make our hearts beat faster, must be from God. It was always in Moses's heart to free his fellow brothers from bondage, and he was called to lead the people of Israel out of Egypt. Your calling in life is already inside of you; it's just a matter of finding who you really are and what passions lie in your heart. Sometimes we feel that since the things we love are secular, they can't be from God.

I would like to tell you my story and how I found my passion in life. I love to cook and bake; however I also love chemistry. Those things are beautiful to me and I am currently pursuing a degree in chemical engineering, which is basically cooking and baking on the industrial scale. I find myself daydreaming about creating the next million-dollar product or finding the cure for cancer. How can I ever glorify God with that? By bringing God into it. The Spirit knows all things, not just theology. I often times ask the Holy Spirit for help in my studies and even on my exams and I receive answers from Him. In this respect, I don't ask God for general help, but I ask specifically what I need help with. I may ask "What is the chemical compound from this NMR spectroscopy?" We don't ask God specific questions because we have made Him out to be a universal intelligence, but He is a Person; He communicates like you and I do, through a love relationship. If we aren't specific with Him, we are not treating Him like a person but rather a universal intelligence. Find that personal time with Him and walk in that manner. When it comes to the workplace, I believe the Holy Spirit will lead me through innovation, creativity and excellence. Your peers will see this and will ask, "How do you do it?" My only answer is Jesus. It is no good to be a "super spiritual" person in the workplace if you cannot do your job. We aren't just to bring God into the marketplace, but we should also be supernaturally extraordinary at our jobs.

God wants you to be released into your destiny with authority and assurance. God needs you to be you; not to be another pastor, but to do what you love to do. Pastors alone aren't going to save the world, but people like you and me, who pursue their calling with excellence. Ephesians 4:11 says, "And He gave some to be apostles, and some as prophets, and some as evangelists, and some as pastors and teachers, for the equipping of the saints for the work of service to the building up of the body of Christ." These are the fivefold ministries, and their role is to equip the saints: you and I. We are supposed to bring God into our spheres of influence. One of the problems continues to be that we believe ministers are higher in the Kingdom than regular Christians. We feel inadequate, as if we are missing God's will in our lives. But the reality is that God is not a respecter of any person, and a person who is in nursing, engineering, business, etc. should be fully assured that the biggest impact they can have in the world is through their sphere of influence.

There would be a great problem if we were all called into church ministry. The church would stay inside the four walls of the church and the world would never know of Jesus. This is a problem of standard Christianity. We aren't being released into our callings with authority. For example, imagine God called you to be an accountant; would you not pursue your work with excellence? You would bring God into your work, asking Him for help, and influencing the people around you. It's time for the church to be released into what they were called to do and get out of the four walls of the church. God belongs in our workplaces.

God gave each of us specific talents and gifts. Let's be proper stewards and glorify Him with those abilities. The book of Colossians illustrates that whatever you do, not just church work, but *whatever you do*, glorify God with it. When the Israelites were building the tabernacle, the Bible says the Holy Spirit fell upon the craftsmen; not the priests, but the *craftsmen*. Let it be a reminder of the love of God for us; He created every human differently, each in his own fashion. I believe the perfect will of God in our lives is to do what God has called us to do, and to glorify Him with it.

Chapter 13
Working the Father Without the Father

A major revelation in my life was realizing that I couldn't accomplish God's assignments unless I continued to remain in fellowship with Him. One might assume that once God gives an assignment, it is all set to run with. In *spiritual reality*, it doesn't work like that. To accomplish God's assignments requires coming back to Him constantly, now more than ever. The fact is that you will not be able to carry out God's assignments without Him. You need Him not just for the birth of it, but throughout the whole process. You need His power, wisdom, and strategy, since He knows all.

During the course of writing this book, I would continually spend time with the Lord. My personal relationship with God was always foremost; it came before this book and anything else in my life. But as I continued to write, I began to get distracted by worldly things. I noticed that when I stepped away from fellowship with him, I immediately lost the brook of living water, from which I got all my revelations. This is because it is through your spirit that you have access to God, and it is out of your spirit that *rivers of living water flow.* It is the Holy Spirit *within* your spirit that gives you the water. So as I kept picking up where I left off in the book, I had no revelation or insight to write about. Up to this point, I wrote what I had not come up with, but rather that which had been revealed to me. Before this, I had no trouble coming up with chapter titles or their content, but when I got distracted and withdrew from His presence, I didn't have the slightest idea of what to write. I thought this would go away. I thought to myself, *surely, revelation isn't that hard to tap into.* I left the writing for a few days at a time, trying to recuperate.

During this time, I did not necessarily return to my fellowship with God, but just lived day-by-day. Then one day, as I was pondering how to keep going, it struck me: *how could I expect to do the things of God without God?* It became crystal clear to me. Some things that we realize don't always come with a "big bang" from God, but rather as *spiritual common sense.* As we grow in our faith, our spirits begin to rule our minds and we see things more clearly because it is not the physical that dictates what happens, but the spiritual. As mentioned in a previous chapter, the secrets of the Lord belong to those who love Him and seek Him wholeheartedly. God will not reveal His work to you unless you stay close to Him. It is *spiritual logic* to know that if you get distracted and step away from God, then how can you expect to hear what God is saying?

I spent the next few days in silent prayer meditating on God's word. I wasn't anxious to continue writing, but rather to bring His presence back into my life. Within days of spending quality time with Him, I began to feel the brook break and water bubble up in my spirit. It is true as it is written in 1 John 5:3 that obeying His commandments really isn't difficult. When we are connected to our source, the work He gives us will flow out of us. In all respects, I was able to keep writing with ease. But this was not a one-time issue that I ran into. I had to keep overcoming it every time I got distracted. Can you imagine what the consequence of getting distracted will be when the Lord will give us assignments greater in size and responsibility? Many of us continue to be where we are in the Lord, because we have not proven ourselves to Him.

> He who is faithful in what is least is faithful also in much; and he who is unjust in what is least is unjust also in much. Therefore if you have not been faithful in the unrighteous mammon, who will commit to your trust the true riches? And if you have not been faithful in what is another man's, who will give you what is your own? (Matthew 16:10-12)

Be encouraged, for the secrets of the Lord belong to those He can trust. Understand that the product of your life is what you have sowed into it. God does not reveal His heart to us immediately. He gives us a little at a time, so that we may learn to steward it. Faithfulness, patience, and character all must cultivate before we receive greater assignments.

The revelation remains to be that we cannot do God's work without God. It is vital to be patient and discern what He is saying. If you do it out of your own vain lust, it will hit dead ends. My desire for this book was to act in faith of what God had spoken to me. I believe I have written down revelation knowledge as received within my spirit, imparted by the Holy Spirit and it is by the grace of God that I was able to relate it. He gives us not only the assignment, but the desire and ability to do it.

For it is God who works in you both to will and to do for His good pleasure. (Philippians 2:13)

He will give us the grace we need to accomplish His will. However it is our job to stay mindful of Him by abiding in His Word and presence. During Jesus' time on earth, He spent countless hours in prayer. He would keep coming back to the presence of the Father. Early in the mornings, he would rise to pray. That is the place where he gained the insight, wisdom and strength to do God's assignments. I once heard a sermon that said Jesus spent all night in prayer before He chose His twelve disciples. We can see throughout the Bible that Jesus not only desired to be with His Father, but also needed the Father's counsel. These secret prayers of Jesus Christ were not written down, because they were prayed from His heart in secret; it is the same for us. The result of our lives will be directly correlated to our personal relationship with Jesus Christ. Our personal relationship with Him is the world's greatest secret.

If God asks you to do something, you're going to need Him like never before. We don't have the capability, wisdom, or power to accomplish His work. If it's of God, it's in need of a divine touch. Therefore, don't be discouraged when something is not working out or seems to be failing. Rather, assess your heart and the time spent with

God. Should you really expect God's involvement if you try to do it all on your own? Can a kingdom run without the king? The kingdom is the abode of the king, and Jesus Christ is the source of His Kingdom. He is the source of wisdom and power, an infinite supply. He does not send us unarmed. We will be equipped with everything we need to bring His will to pass, but you will need to spend continual time with Him, and even more so when He entrusts a work to you.

To say, "Why doesn't God just let me do it," is very illogical thinking. Here's a small illustration. Let's say you're in line at Wal-Mart and God tells you to tell the cashier that He loves her so much! You think to yourself, *why should I say "God loves you so much" if I can simply say "God loves you"*? As you pay for your merchandise, you turn and say, "God loves you!" The cashier gives a warm response and seems to be blessed by it, but deep within the woman is not satisfied at all. She's been searching for God all her life; she's always heard the common phrase, 'God loves you,' but she's been asking God to tell her in a more personal way. God had sent an answer to meet her need, but because you trusted your way over God's, she was unable to hear what God wanted to speak to her.

Our thoughts can always create an alternative, but we don't know the person or situation that God wants to touch. It is imperative to obey every word that God gives us. More than that, we have to follow His strategy to bring about the result He desires. He knows what yields the best result. God alone knows the needs of His people and is ready to meet them. I highly suggest you let the Father guide you in His own work!

Chapter 14
Living Out of His Presence

There was a time in my life when the routine of everyday responsibility overwhelmed me. School and ministry consumed me, and I had lost sight of the true reason why I was doing those things in the first place. We have all experienced this in our lives. I understood God didn't want me to live stressed, but I had no idea what to do with these emotions. I began to tell God about all that was happening. I was searching for justification, desiring God's peace and purpose to fill my heart. In the following moments, I found myself reading this psalm:

I will walk before the Lord in the land of the living. (Psalm 116:9)

Immediately I understood God was saying, "Live out of My presence and by what I have spoken to you." God began to show me that He does not call us to live a life of peace by our own abilities. He desires us to always be at peace, but this will only come from a personal relationship with Him. It is in His presence where we find joy, peace, and confidence. When you live from His presence, you are accepting the direction He has for you and His Word as the truth for your life. Most men and women walk in the vanity of their imagination, but God says, "No, stop! You are ruining your life! Come back to Me and you will find peace!"

I personally believe that the best part of Jesus' day was when He was with His Father. It was not healing the sick or casting out demons that gave him the most joy; it was the Father who anointed Him with gladness (Hebrews 1:9). Jesus spent hours in prayer and worship, adoring the Father. He loved Him (Matthew 11:25), and Jesus' love for the Father caused Him to do all that the Father asked of Him. If Jesus Himself needed His Father's presence, how much more do we need Him? When Jesus said, *"Do not rejoice that you can cast out demons in My Name, but that your names are written in the Lamb's Book of Life"* (Luke 10:20), He was reminding us to keep our minds and hearts on what's important. He put priority and value on knowing the Father. All that He did, He did because of the Father; He would move as the Father moved and He would speak as the Father spoke.

So how do we live from His Presence? We need to have an ever-increasing relationship with Him. Spend time seeking Him through prayer and worship. When you find Him, you are able to imitate Him, but you must keep coming back to His presence. Jesus would continually go back to the Father. No matter what happened on any given day, Jesus sought the Father. There were moments when Jesus wanted to depart from the crowds, so that He could rest in His Father's presence (Luke 4:42). Not only does God's presence give us power and wisdom, but also it restores our strength.

Resting is entering the actual presence of God, which is not quickly done because we are so pre-occupied with our lives. However, it is easy to enter His presence if we come focused and contrite in heart. When we enter His presence and *rest* even for a moment, we are strengthened immensely. A moment in His rest is equivalent to a full day's natural rest. That is not doctrine, but simply a comparison for the natural mind to understand.

We know that God was speaking to Jesus because Jesus constantly reiterated that "I say and do what I see the Father doing" (John 5:30). You will not have the proper direction or ability to perform acts of God without taking the time to know Him. When you take those steps to know Him, you will come to a place of true rest, which will give you peace, joy and righteousness (Romans 14:17). This is the quality of life God desires for us.

Imagine a time when you felt the tangible Presence of God and you experienced peace. You felt it linger even when you left your prayer room but did it permanently stay? If we don't make His presence a constant practice in our lives, this peace will come and go. This applies to any fruit of the Spirit, whether it is love, joy, peace, patience, kindness, goodness, faithfulness, gentleness, or self-control. Jesus possessed all of these fruits. He lived by His spirit. Though He operated from His spirit, He was also God. He was of pure virtue. In this way, Jesus is both like us and completely unlike us. We are like him by way of our spirits, which were made righteous by His blood. As we become spiritually minded, we will experience the birth of these fruits in our lives.

We often hear, "It is already within us," however, we must understand that it has to be activated. When you are saved, there is no doubt you are perfect in your spirit, but it is your soul that needs to be renewed to experience the life of the Spirit. If these activations are not triggered in a Christian's life, they can go their whole life without ever tasting life in the Spirit.

Bear in mind that when I speak of your spirit, I am also implying the fact that the Holy Spirit is already within you, so don't misjudge when I mention only your spirit and not God. If you are born-again, God already lives in your spirit. Jesus was led by the Spirit, as we ought to be; He was spiritually minded.

When we gaze upon Jesus, we are transformed into His image. What I am suggesting here may be personal theory, but the deeper I go in my walk with God, the more I experience this to be true. I have realized that one cannot become like Christ unless they see Christ. This is affirmed in 2 Corinthians 3:18, *But we all, with unveiled face, beholding as in a mirror the glory of the Lord, are being transformed into the same image from glory to glory, just as by the Spirit of the Lord.* As mentioned earlier, true sight and belief is not found in our physical eyes, but in our spiritual eyes. It is within our spirit that we experience the fullness of God, and it is our heart that can see Christ. Some may immediately write this off as an imaginative way of explaining God, but I am not suggesting that at all. I am suggesting the *science* behind Christianity.

Many assume that Christianity is a systematic structure of beliefs founded on faith alone. Christianity however is the deepest form of science the world has yet to discover. The reality of the spiritual world is a phenomenon to the world. There are numerous supernatural encounters that the world doesn't understand. It is foolishness to keep living without having answers to the unexplained. I believe God is no fan of delusion. He is not trying to keep the world in a mystery about His existence, but the fact is that flesh is flesh and spirit is spirit. One cannot understand the Spirit, or the things of God, without being born of the Spirit (John 3:6).

In other words, spiritual reality will remain to be a mystery to the world, because they are spiritually inoperative. Their spirits remain to be present within their bodies, but they are *dead* spirits. I am not suggesting that they are dead people. In Genesis, God told Adam he would die if he ate of the forbidden fruit. Adam's spirit indeed did die after he ate of the fruit, but this death was not physical as we know it. No spirit will ever cease to exist; Spirit is eternal. If you are still breathing, born-again or not, you possess a spirit. When a person dies, their spirit leaves their body. Therefore, the *dead in spirit* refers to people cut off from the righteousness of God. Their spirits will pay the penalty for not putting their trust in Jesus Christ. Jesus is able to redeem any spirit, but if one does not believe with their heart unto righteousness (Romans 10:10), they will remain a *dead* spirit.

With the same heart, we are to look upon Christ. My theory continues to be that as I spend time in prayer and worship, I am in the very presence of Jesus Christ; but because my spiritual eyes are not fully developed, I am unable to make out Christ. I experience Him as if He is literally there, and it is because He *is* there. We are able to look upon "the Man" Jesus Christ with our spirit man. We have access to the Throne of God by spirit. This may be hard to understand, but keep these things in your heart and they shall prove themselves to be true. Search the scriptures and you shall experience the spiritual truths that we don't understand until we become spiritually minded.

Remember, this all happens because the Holy Spirit dwells within us. He gives us the ability to be spiritually minded. It is God who wills and God who does (Philippians 2:13); there is nothing apart from Him. He is the air you breathe and the steps you take. He exists in all and through all (Ephesians 4:6). My impression continues to be that we cannot become aware of our new identity in Christ unless we are aware of Christ Himself. We are made aware of Christ when we see Him. How do we see Jesus if He is not physically present? We see Him in our spirit man. There are many references in scripture that point to this truth.

> *But we all, with unveiled face, beholding as in a mirror the glory of the Lord, are being transformed into the same image from glory to glory, just as by the Spirit of the Lord.* (2 Corinthians 3:18)

> *Beloved, now we are children of God; and it has not yet been revealed what we shall be, but we know that when He is revealed, we shall be like Him, for we shall see Him as He is.* (1 John 3:2)

> *When Christ who is our life appears, then you also will appear with Him in glory.* (Colossians 3:4)

When we spend time in His presence, we are transformed. We don't experience the fruits of the Spirit simply for the sake of experiencing them. God gives us a taste of the fruit of the Spirit so we can come to a place of permanency. He wants those virtues to be birthed fully within us. When the fruit of the Spirit grows within you, you begin to live in a quality of life as it is in the Presence of God. A person who lives from the Presence of God will embody the following characteristics.

> *One thing I do, forgetting those things, which are behind, and reaching forward to those things, which are ahead. I press toward the goal for the prize of the upward call of God in Christ Jesus.*
> (Philippians 3:13-14)

> *For our citizenship is in heaven, from which we also eagerly wait for the Savior, the Lord Jesus Christ.* (Philippians 3:20)

> *Set your affection on things above, not below.* (Colossians 3:2)

> *Be anxious for nothing, but in everything by prayer and supplication, with thanksgiving.* (Philippians 4:6)

> *And the peace of God, which surpasses all understanding, will guard your hearts and minds through Jesus Christ.* (Philippians 4:7)

These are amazing traits to have. Can you imagine being wholeheartedly excited for the cause of Christ? He doesn't just make us feel alive, but He literally gives us life.

God commanded us to bring His kingdom to earth; this not done naturally because that proves nothing. When we live supernatural lives, we can prove the reality of God. We are to show the world that life in Christ is much better than any other life. There is nothing that can surpass the satisfaction of the love of God when you are fully immersed in it. I am truly convinced that nothing will ever overcome sin in our lives except the satisfaction of the love of God. One can give up sin for a short while, but he will need to search for other pleasures. God is not interested in leaving us orphans, without food or home. Rather, He invites us into His kingdom where there is a surplus of food. When you allow God to pour His love out on you, you will have no desire to sin. As we have shared in His death, we are to share in His new life. We are called of the same inheritance. We should no longer walk in vanity as the world does, but as a royal priesthood enthroned in heavenly places with Jesus Christ.

Chapter 15
Living in His Domain

God Conscious vs. Man Conscious

I have had numerous conversations with people where I completely lost track of what they were saying. I was physically present but not at all able to remember what was said. I have also been at numerous social events where I did not converse with some people because I didn't seek them out. I had made a decision to be unaware of them. Subconsciously or consciously, we make daily decisions about whether or not we will be conscious of God.

God does speak to His people every day. He is always around them, wherever they go. He observes them in their daily activities, as they go in and out of places. He is constantly revealing Himself, but most don't ever encounter Him because they aren't paying attention to Him. You cannot have a relationship with someone you are not aware of. You will be unable to see Him unless you are, in fact, conscious of Him. Furthermore, you cannot go where God is going if you don't actually see where He is leading you. Therefore, you cannot experience God in your life if you are not where He wants you to be. This is the opposite of living in His domain. God's *domain* is the place of His provision and grace for your life. It is where you want to be to fully experience God. As many often wonder, I asked God, "How come I don't see Your hand in my life as often as I should?" It was then that I heard the Holy Spirit say, "Because you're not in My *domain*." I was brought back to the story of Elijah hiding in a cave in fear of Queen Jezebel.

> *And Ahab told Jezebel all that Elijah had done also how he had executed all the prophets with the sword. Then Jezebel sent a messenger to Elijah saying, "So let the gods do to me, and more also, if I do not make your life as the life of one of them by tomorrow about this time." And when he saw that, he arose and ran for his life.*

> *And there he went into a cave, and spent the night in that place; and behold, the word of the Lord came to him, and He said to him, "**What are you doing here, Elijah?**"* (1 Kings 19)

God was confronting Elijah about his whereabouts, while at the same time questioning the condition of his heart. This is consistent with God's nature throughout the Bible, where we find God questioning man's intentions. When Adam and Eve hid in the garden after they ate of the forbidden fruit, God asked, "Where are you Adam?" Similarly, God asked Peter, "Do you love me?" which begs the question, why would God ask questions He already knows the answer to? It is for the purpose of the work of the Holy Spirit. These questions go out from the mouth of God to change our hearts. When we step away from Him, He calls us back. When our hearts fail to understand, He shines His light. This is the work of the Spirit of God. His words carry power and life. When you hear a *Holy Spirit question,* you should know there is growth coming. You may hear these questions daily, weekly or monthly. This is not a doctrine or a theological concept. It varies upon individual. Remember, no man sees the work of God within another man. He is a *whirlwind* invisible to the naked eye.

> *The wind blows where it wishes, and you hear the sound of it, but cannot tell where comes from and where it goes. So is everyone who is born of the Spirit.* (John 3:6-8)

There are many other ways God works in your life, but one of those ways is through Holy Spirit *questions.* They are directed at you and meant for your growth. They are meant to bring you to a higher place. When the Holy Spirit asks you a question, you should realize two things: one, He already knows the answer and two, there is a purpose for that question. If He knows the answer, then it's all about you "figuring it out." God gets it, but He asks the question so that *you* can get it. God asked Elijah why he was hiding in the cave because Elijah was not supposed to be hiding. He ran to the cave in fear of Queen Jezebel who vowed to kill him. He had left God's provision. God understood Elijah was afraid, but He needed Elijah to realize his fault in not trusting Him. Through the process, Elijah not only grew in faith, but was able to furthermore walk in victory and peace. If you trust God, then regardless of what you face you will be content in His provision and abundance of peace.

Another example of this divine inquiry was Jesus asking Peter if He loved Him (John 21:15-19). Up to that point, Peter did not fully understand what it meant to be saved by grace. I will mention three occurrences in Peter's life that show this. The first one was at the Transfiguration; Peter interrupted the presence of God by saying, "Let us build three memorials here, one for You, Moses and Elijah," but God overshadowed Peter, declaring, "This is my beloved Son in whom I am well pleased. Hear Him" (Luke 9:28). Another time Peter vowed to Jesus that he would never deny Him, but assuredly he did, three times! This continued to show Peter's misunderstanding of the gospel of grace. Then a final time, Peter's zeal led him to cut off one of the servants' ears in the Garden of Gethsemane, but Jesus rebuked Him for it. These were all incidents where Peter's self righteousness got the better of him. He did not understand what Jesus was all about. He did not understand that it was not his zeal that would carry the gospel of love, but God's. Peter had been operating out of a *saved by works* mentality, which caused him to do all those self-righteous acts. But on the shore of the Sea of Galilee, Jesus restored Peter's heart. Peter did not understand the truth until Jesus spoke three times prophetically, cutting to the root of Peter's heart. Jesus asked Peter whether he loved Him so that he could get him to understand that it was all about God's love, the love that would essentially *take care of and feed the sheep*, and not humanistic love. Peter began to understand the message of the gospel, *for it is by grace that we are saved and nothing of our doing* (Ephesians 2:8-9).

In the same way, the Holy Spirit asks us questions to help us realize His will in our hearts. How does a man's heart change and turn to the

Will of God? It does so when the Holy Spirit speaks to us. His words carry power and life. When God asks you a question, can you imagine what it does to you? It causes you to think and struggle within yourself, trying to realize what God is speaking to you. Eventually, you will find the answer. The question the Spirit asks is directed towards that area of your heart that needs to be unraveled. When we begin to answer the question, we realize what needs to be surrendered. We also start to see what the Lord wants us to do. In most cases, it is a character adjustment or a change in perspective. These questions shed light on our minds, revealing the matters of our hearts.

When the Lord told me I was not living in His domain, I began to realize how Elijah had stepped out of God's domain and saw his provision cease. I then realized, "How could I expect to see God if I am not where He is?" I understood that if I wanted to experience God in my life, I have to be where He wants me to be.

Our great example, Jesus, was always where His Father wanted Him. He always did what His Father asked of Him. He walked in God's provision, performing miracles upon miracles and fulfilling His Father's will. You and I are meant to be like Jesus. We are nothing less. *We have the mind of Christ* (1 Corinthians 2:16) and are *made His Righteousness* (2 Corinthians 5:21). Many Christians assume that Jesus was God and that's the end of it. They forget that He also was a man. They acknowledge He was a man, but when it comes down to their own walks with God, they do not use Jesus as their perfect example. Instead, they choose from a variety of Christian acquaintances. People choose not to make Jesus their example because then they would have to live up to a perfect standard. They don't want to accept that personal responsibility for the way they should be living.

It all comes down to what you decide. *You* make a decision to be ignorant of God. *You* make a decision to look up to other Christians. But Jesus Christ not only was, but also continues to be our Standard. To further prove that God does expect you to use Jesus as your example, we can look at what qualifies Him to be our example.

Therefore He is also able to save to the uttermost those who come to God through Him, since He always lives to make intercession for them. (Hebrews 7:25)

Jesus is able to be our example because He intercedes on our behalf; only those that went through the same trials and tribulations can rightfully speak on your behalf. Jesus was tempted in every point as we are, yet did not sin (Hebrews 4:15). He was tempted not only to commit physical sin, but to be depressed and discouraged. He was tempted to be passive and lazy. He was tempted to be angry. Yet, He did not give Himself into temptation for the sake of the world. For your sake He withstood temptation.

For we do not have a High Priest who cannot sympathize with our weaknesses, but was in all points tempted as we are, yet without sin. (Hebrews 4:15)

We have to acknowledge that Jesus was human and had to deal with life just like we do on a daily basis. Only when we understand this are we able to look up to Jesus completely, knowing He was once "in our shoes." We must see that as Christians we are "little Christ's" on earth. We have all the abilities to represent Jesus Christ as He was. So when it comes to struggling with sin in our lives, there is no excuse for it. If Jesus overcame it, you can overcome it. If Jesus conquered it, you can conquer it (John 16:33). It is important to remember that you have already conquered the issue; you just need to activate that spirit mindedness which is already within you and exercise authority over it.

Finances

Jesus was an example to both the materialistically rich and poor. I would often wonder why Jesus wasn't necessarily a rich man. Many religious people love to use that argument against prosperity. In reality, Jesus had all He needed. Do we find any reference in scripture where Jesus needed something but couldn't have it? No. He knew the Creator and He knew that His supply came directly from Him. He trusted God to meet all His needs and God did. Jesus had no problem in the financial aspect of His life, because He simply knew God would provide.

The point I am making is that Jesus was an example to both the rich and the poor. He showed His trust in God by not needing to carry a 401k in His pocket. He showed that man didn't need to worry about money. I am not implying you shouldn't save money. I am saying that Jesus was not necessarily rich, to prove to both the rich man and poor man that with God, money is the least of issues. He showed us that He never had lack of money, nor did He show that He was wealthy. Both the rich man and the poor man idealize wealth. Because even when the poor believe God is against prosperity and money is evil, they are making money of importance in their lives. But God is saying, "Money has nothing to do with it! I am the priority in your life! Don't give money that power over you!" By saying it is either completely evil or good, you are idolizing it. Jesus does not stand in the way of money; rather, He puts it into its place. He shows us that it is all about Him. The amount of finances you have does not define your wealth. It is your supply that defines your wealth.

Road of Mercy and Provision

There are two roads for the Christian. He can choose to walk the *road of mercy* or the *road of provision and favor*. I believe those who are born-again step off the course of destruction and onto the course of mercy. However, the course of mercy is only the foundation. In addition, we are meant to walk on the course of provision. Sadly, many standard Christians never experience the road of provision and favor because they continue to walk in their own will. God's *domain* is in His will and He is able to provide in that place. If we walk according to our own lusts, we will not experience God's favor and grace.

Too many Christians have settled for the road of mercy, where they live for both worlds. They are content with being "saved," but the fruit of salvation is growth. We must walk in the place God has prepared and designed for us. When we do this, we will bring glory to Him and success into our lives. We must return to the Father's house!

†

Chapter 16
Breaking the Threshold

Radical change requires radical *voices*. A system that has been in a traditional routine will not change on its own, nor will it change quickly. This can apply to your local church, workplace, or any sphere of influence you are a part of. To break the threshold of routine, there are two principles of radical change we must understand.

1. *Change requires action*

2. *A collection of 'voices' brings radical change*

As we assess the environments we are a part of every day, we will find that these two principles are the potential drivers of change. In many local churches today, there is a fear of change, and the masses force the individuals that want change to step back. This also applies to any aspect of life. When you try to change an environment that has been stable and going in one direction for a long period of time, you most definitely will face opposition. Today, there are more people that live in fear instead of love. It is the common nature of sin. Sin brought evil into the world and ever since then, along with many other heinous vices, fear rules the people. But the Word of God says, "perfect love casts out fear" (1 John 4:18). There is nothing more beautiful than when man meets the love of God. It removes fear from his life. He is able to walk fearless into the enemy's camp, as Joshua did with Jericho. We must obtain the love of God before we break any threshold.

Keep in mind; your agenda is not to break the threshold, but to obey every word that comes from the mouth of God (Matthew 4:4). When you follow God's orders, you will see the *walls of Jericho* fall. Whatever God desires in your sphere of influence will come to pass when you join Him in His work. It is through you that He will accomplish His will. You are the voice that He will use. In the context of this book, a *voice* refers to the individual who does what God called him or her to do. On earth, God fulfills His purposes through *voices*. He has designed each of us in such a way that we are fully capable of bringing His kingdom to earth. To whatever sphere of influence God has called you, it is there that you must be a *voice*. Every *voice* will be prophetic, breaking the threshold of routine and tradition.

> *So shall My word be that goes forth from My mouth; It shall not return to Me void, but it shall accomplish what I please, and it shall prosper in the thing for which I sent it.* (Isaiah 55:11)

As you begin to release what God has spoken to you, you will always experience results. God knows the need and He sends a word to satisfy that need. Jesus was always successful when He released God's *word*. He never found the *word* coming back to Him void and without effect. Lazarus did come out of the grave when Jesus commanded him to (John 11:43) and every time He spoke, His *word* was satisfied by a positive response. Lepers were healed, blind eyes were opened, and so on. We have the same potential to be like Jesus!

The question some may ask is *what will happen if only one person responds to God's will?* One voice is louder than a thousand silent voices, and the threshold will break regardless. God's word can shake the earth ten times before you blink once. He needs no extra strength to do so. He has all the power in the world, but He needs to carry out His purposes through us. In the physical world, flesh institutes a vessel of authority. When God gave Adam authority over all things on earth, He gave it for all time. Therefore, Jesus had to come *in the flesh* to exercise His righteousness over corrupt flesh; we as children of God have been given Godly authority. It is through our bodies that God's power can be released on earth. God could not redeem us from heaven, but had to come down to earth, so He also cannot do from heaven what He has given us the authority to do on earth. However without Him, we are completely hopeless. It is essentially His power within us that can change things. Therefore, as voices of God, we are the salt and light of the world. We expose the darkness, and it is our light that will break the customs and patterns of the world, bringing the Kingdom of God to earth.

> *You are the light of the world. A town built on a hill cannot be hidden.* (Matthew 5:14)

Wherever you are called to by God, do so with confidence and faith; your *words* will bring prosperous results. Even if no one joins you in the work, you will have a tremendous impact. It is like when a lamp is lit in a dark room—everyone who walks into the room will see it. In your work, both believers and unbelievers will notice God working through you (John 13:35).

To further illustrate the point let's look at Jesus, the one Man responsible for our redemption. Two thousand years ago, one man responded to what God told Him to do. Today, Christianity remains the largest religion in the world. Despite all the opposition the church faced, outside and within, Christianity continues to claim a third of the world's population. Jesus impacted the world because He was a *voice*, fulfilling everything God told Him to do.

Now, someone may completely overlook that and say Jesus is an exception, because He was God. Though that is true, Jesus made a statement that challenges that notion, *"Most assuredly, I say to you, he who believes in Me, the works that I do he will do also; and greater works than these he will do, because I go to My Father"* (John 14:12). If we make the argument that His voice only had an impact because He was God, then what Jesus stated is irrelevant. Jesus said, *"What I did, you will do and even greater!"* Jesus was challenging us and essentially saying, "No more excuses! I've given you My word, now go and do something with it! My word will not return to Me void."

You cannot look past the responsibility God has placed upon your life simply because you don't believe you can do it. You will answer according to His Word. He was speaking to you, two thousand years ago, breaking through time; His Word is eternal and true. My point in saying all this is that you need to move forward in what God has called you to. You can no longer ignore it. You have no one to blame and no excuse to make. You will answer to Jesus and Jesus alone. He will point to His Word and say, "Did I not tell you that you will do greater works than I" (John 14:12)?

Children of God, let's enter into our glorious inheritance and be done with the patterns of the world. His kingdom has so much more to offer! If you can imagine a place of no hurt or chaos, you're going to love heaven. The Kingdom of God *is* the quality of life that awaits us in heaven. God's plan is to give us a taste of that life now.

We as the body of Christ have the duty and responsibility to reveal the power of God. He commanded His church to represent Him (Mark 16:15). We as a church are a corporate body. Jesus Christ on earth was limited to His individual body. He was unable to be everywhere but as His body we are many in number. If you understood everything I have said to this point, you can conclude that Jesus Christ simply multiplied Himself to the world. We are His multiplication. Jesus established His body to fulfill His purpose. It is evident to me that the body of Christ is meant to be the very same thing as Jesus Himself being on earth. Jesus didn't stay on earth because He would be unable to fulfill His purpose as one man. He said however, *"Nevertheless I tell you the truth. It is to your advantage that I go away; for if I do not go away, the Helper will not come to you; but if I depart, I will send Him to you"* (John 16:7). I am not demoting Jesus at all, because the Holy Spirit being present on earth is in fact Jesus the Spirit form, for God is one. He now lives in every believer. That's amazing! By sending the Holy Spirit, Jesus was saying, "I must go so the church can do its work through the power of My Spirit." He was also saying, "I am not able fulfill My Purpose without My body." The purpose of Jesus' death was redemption and to give us a purpose. He gave His church a purpose to carry His name to all nations. He needed to go to the Father to send the Holy Spirit forward for this reason. First Jesus came to earth to redeem us, leaving only to return through the Holy Spirit, and He will come back again to liberate us wholly, uniting spirit, soul, and body. He painted a beautiful love story that will resonate for all eternity.

Corporate level of change is the result of singular change. It begins at the individual level. I mentioned that you shouldn't worry if others join you in God's work, but there is yet another secret to that. Your one voice will be appealing and contagious to those around you. Your light will influence people. As a child of God, you have more weight and authority over any darkness that may cover people. You can subdue any stronghold in a person's life. However when a stronghold is cast down in one's life, they will have a choice to make. They will have to decide to choose victory over it, or be drawn again towards it. If one does not willingly reject a stronghold, they will be giving it power over them (Romans 6:16; Galatians 5:1). But a born-again believer has already been freed from such powers and has authority over any spiritual foe if he exercises it. It is true when the Bible says, "If God is for you, who can stand against you" (Romans 8:31).

Therefore, as you pursue God's will, people will notice that there is something bigger than you at work, because they will know that no human has the ability, strength, endurance, power, wisdom, or strategy, to the magnitude that God will uncover in your life. Many will turn and open their hearts to God; uniting with you in the work God has called you to. It is then that the second principle of radical change comes into effect; a collection of *voices* bringing radical change. This is very applicable to local churches. If we want God to visit church services across the nation, there must be a corporate response of hunger, honor, and devotion.

I am challenging you today to assess the current condition of your heart. Do you want the healing and manifest presence of God to come where you are? Do you want to experience this in your local church? Do you want this to be noticed at your workplace? It requires a corporate level of change. Even a few *voices* joined together are much louder than any amount of silent voices. Therefore, don't be afraid to step out in faith. God will be faithful to His Word; He has esteemed His Word above His own name (Psalm 138:2). When He speaks to you, be bold as a lion and speak it.

Before any radical change can occur, action must be taken (principle #1). In a corporation, the CEO and board of directors have the job of leading the company in a strategic vision, but before the company can move in a new direction, a decision must be made that involves strategy. It is only when the decision is made that action follows, turning the company in a new direction.

It is the same with a church. To begin moving in a new direction, *voices* need to rise up. A people fulfilling His will need to arise from the ashes. We wait for revivals, but revival is simply God having His place in our meetings. This isn't up to God, but up to us as individual Christians to respond to God's voice. There is very little time left; eternity is right around the corner. There is no more time to delay what God has spoken to you. Begin to move in what He speaks to you, because until you do, you will get nowhere.

In my personal life, it was not until I made a step of faith, a decision, to move in what God had spoken to me that I saw breakthrough. I saw my faith grow, and I began to experience God all around me. As I journeyed with God, I began to realize that fearing risk and change wasn't even worth it. I realized that fear is a lie; it is an illusion of the devil persuading people to delay God's plans. Satan scares us from our own authority over Him. It is ludicrous to live in fear of someone under you. It is in our personal relationship with Jesus that we conquer this fear. We may still experience fear, but as we become closer to Jesus we will not focus on fear but on Him. In all we go through, we will be at peace because His rod and staff comfort us (Psalm 23:4). We may not always find our circumstances comfortable, but we can always find comfort in the One we're with. His name is Love and He is the most wonderful Person in the world. He will bring you to a place of rest, where the world does not worry you. He will place eternity in your heart, and as your perspective changes you will gain love and passion. Leave it all in His hands.

For it is God who works in you both to will and to do for His good pleasure. (Philippians 2:13)

Chapter 17
The Missing Generation

There is a generation today that is missing. This is a generation of Godly saints, young men and women that never reached their mark. This is a generation the Lord wept over, a generation that lost its place in history. A lost generation leaves the next generation barren and without hope. As a family is strengthened throughout its generations, so is the body of Christ. Rather than giving hope and exemplifying a life in Christ, the missing generation has nothing to show for the Kingdom of God. It leaves the next generation with a dilemma. What does a righteous generation really look like? Is it really possible to live a powerful, influential life as a Christian? There is no hope in blaming the previous generation. On the contrary, the current generation must challenge itself to come back to the Word of God.

> He shall be like a tree planted by the rivers of water, that brings forth its fruit in its season, whose leaf also shall not wither; and whatever he does shall prosper. (Psalm 1:3 (See also Jeremiah 17:8))

The Bible reveals the potential of a righteous generation, one that will prosper in every way. I am not writing off the previous generation as having done nothing for the Kingdom. The Lord fulfilled His will with those who loved Him, but I will not grant them the glory of Christ as having fulfilled His perfect will for their generation. What I see around me are youth that feel God is distant. They feel God does not speak today and is not near to them because Christians around them have not been good examples. I say this with great sensitivity of heart. The generations before us have brought us to where we are. The church has made great strides, because God does fulfill His purposes. I am not proclaiming that everything has been lost to this point, not at all. I am however putting the responsibility back on us, as Christians, to become *voices* in this world, to be examples to our children, and to raise righteous generations.

There are many icons for the Kingdom that we see in various spheres of influence, but it is not enough. The majority of Christians do not walk in God's will. One may say, "At least something is being done," but that will never be enough. Thus, we see such a poor representation of Christianity in society. We are seen as religious bigots for the most part; we say we believe in God but we live just like the world. If we don't walk in His will, we are merely following our own egos. God has no part in such hearts. The biggest evidence of one's Christianity is love (John 13:35). Do you love all people equally, in and out of church? Do you open your arms to outsiders the same you would to friends? Do you love God with all your heart, soul, strength and mind (Luke 10:27)?

My intention is not to put blame on any generation, but to place the responsibility back on us for the next generation. The current generation has the responsibility of upbringing the next generation. If we live supernatural lives, we will set up the coming generation for the same. We will discipline them to be seekers of God and it will be common knowledge that God speaks. But today even Christians, let alone unbelievers, hardly believe in an intimate relationship with God. But it is *all about* your love relationship with Him. We should be engaging with God on a daily basis.

> *God did this so that they would seek him and perhaps reach out*
> *for him and find him, though he is not far from any one of us.*
> (Acts 17:27)

I have always been a passionate advocate for youth to realize how real God is. I thank God that by His grace, at a very young age, I was able to understand His reality and how close He was to me. I understood that no matter what pleasure I would experience, nothing would compare to experiencing Him. And so I have always advocated strongly for youth because they grow up believing life is better lived chasing after the lusts of this world. How little they realize. It angers and saddens me to see young people that have not had the proper upbringing from the previous generation to know the reality of a living God. The greatest phenomenon in the world continues to be the ignorance of the reality of God. I for one want greater for my generation. I want my generation to prove the acceptable, pleasing and perfect will of God (Romans 12:2). Not everyone may answer the call, but it is not an acceptable alternative to simply *believe* for a response. We must stand alert in faith, bringing His kingdom to earth, knowing we have God Almighty standing behind us. When we act in this confidence, people will notice God behind the scenes.

When people see a generation that reflects the very image of God, they will seek after Him. Every person in the world has an innate desire for spiritual matters. It is essentially because every living being is made of Spirit. Spirit is the evidence of life. It is God who first was. You cannot separate God from man, for God breathed His own breath into man to make him alive. It is not God who is the problem; rather it is Christians' poor reflection of God that does not convince the world of the reality of God. We can have a much greater influence in the world than we currently do. Jesus said to bring His kingdom to earth, implying it is possible and our very purpose. When we begin to walk in His glory, nations will seek after us.

With all that said, reflect upon these things: in five, ten years, where will you be? Do you believe God is indeed GOD? Being a regular church-going Christian will fade away. There will come a time in your life when the Lord Jesus Christ will come to the door of your heart and ask you once again, "Have you rejected yourself and chosen Me?" There will come a point in your life where you will no longer be able to lie to yourself about what truly lives inside of you. If Christ doesn't have the throne of your life, you will assuredly see your own reign come to an end. At that point, you will either continue to deny the truth in ignorance and pride, or you will fall down to the feet of the One who so loved you; the One who broke His flesh for you. His name is Jesus Christ.

I am the way, the truth, and the life. (John 14:6)

✝

A look into "The World's Greatest Secret"

I once told an atheist man that God loved Him. He looked at me blankly, and he stated defensively that He only believed in what he could see and experience. Without losing a beat, the Holy Spirit spoke to me, saying, "Flesh is flesh and Spirit is spirit" (John 3:6-8). The mystery this man didn't understand was that only those reborn of the Spirit could comprehend spiritual things. This man could not rely on his own understanding, because flesh understands only the things of the flesh. This is why God teaches us to trust Him by faith.

It is in silence that man finds God and God finds man. It is our spirits that redeem our souls, because that's where the Holy Spirit resides. However, the Spirit cannot work within you if you live carnally minded. If you feed the flesh, you will starve the spirit. But if you feed the spirit, you will starve the flesh. Spiritual truth tends to be hard to understand, because only the spirit can discern spiritual truth. If we want to be changed, we must come to God by way of our spirits. As we open our hearts to Him, our souls are exposed and He is able to come in and touch us. He comes in and heals every wound. He exposes every thought of unbelief. He takes captive what does not belong in our hearts. This is the work of the Holy Spirit.

This secret place, in the very presence of God, is what allows you to acquire spiritual position. You are already seated with Christ in spirit (Ephesians 2:6), but it will not be activated until you draw from it. It will be from this Place that you acquire divine wisdom and knowledge. It is from the Secret Place that you learn to hear and do as God wills. As you come to know the will of God, you will gain that intimate knowledge that can only come from soaking in His presence in the Secret Place. Whether you fulfill God's will or not, the Secret Place will remain to be a mystery. No one in the flesh can see the Spirit of God, yet He works and does for His good pleasure (Philippians 2:13). Those who join Him will perform extraordinary deeds that only God can be the author of. This partnership will lead to a beautiful and extraordinary life, abundant in joy and peace, proving the perfect will of God.

We will only activate that spiritual stature when we seek Him wholeheartedly. We discover Him in the Secret Place, in that deep, mysterious part of us that truly is the world's greatest secret...

Coming 2013